HIZZY

THE AUTOBIOGRAPHY OF
STEVE HISLOP 1962–2003

with STUART BARKER

CollinsWillow

An Imprint of HarperCollins*Publishers*

First published in Great Britain in 2003
by CollinsWillow
an imprint of HarperCollins*Publishers* London

This paperback edition first published in 2004

1 3 5 7 9 8 6 4 2

A CIP catalogue record for this book is
available from the British Library

The HarperCollins website address is:
www.harpercollins.co.uk

ISBN 0-00-771341-X

Typeset by Rowland Phototypesetting Ltd,
Bury St Edmunds, Suffolk
Printed and bound in Great Britain
by Bookmarque Ltd, Croydon, Surrey

Contents

Foreword

In the summer of 2002, Steve Hislop and I sat down at a blank computer screen at the beginning of a journey to tell his incredible life story. Despite the dangers of his profession, I never once imagined that I would have to finish the journey alone.

Like so many others, I was completely devastated to receive the news that Hizzy had been killed in a helicopter crash on Wednesday, 30 July 2003. The hardback version of the book we had written together had been released just one month before and I know Steve was very proud of it so there was at least some consolation in knowing that Hizzy had lived long enough to commit his life story to paper so his exploits could be read about by future generations. In that sense, as well as through the videos and photographs we have of him, he will never be forgotten.

For the launch of the paperback version of *Hizzy* in 2004, Steve and I were contracted to script an additional chapter to bring it up to date. Following his death, this task fell to me alone. Waking up every day to write about someone you have so recently lost is no easy task and I said on more than one occasion that if all writing was as difficult as that I would find another job.

I missed Steve's critical input and his incredible memory for detail and I missed seeing his face light up when he recalled episodes from his past that even he thought he had forgotten. But mostly I missed the laughs we had sipping a few beers and chatting about his past. Coming from the same part of the world as me, Steve had been a hero of mine for 16 years before I actually got to know him well which made things even more special for me; after all, it's not every day your hero becomes your friend.

The book you are holding now is a special edition which contains a selection of chapters from the full-length *CollinsWillow* paperback. I have tried to choose chapters spanning the length of Steve's career from his childhood through his first race wins and from his years as a major road racing star to his untimely death. Every chapter up to chapter 16 is the work Steve and I did together before that fateful day. The final two chapters are my work alone and I can only hope I have done Steve justice in finishing his story.

Hizzy's life was plagued with tragedy and ill fortune and it was only because of his incredible resilience and fighting spirit that there were passages of great triumph and joy to balance things out. His was a life worth living and therefore a life worth remembering and I am extremely proud to have been involved in its telling. This one's for you Stevie . . .

Stuart Barker

Day Number One,
Life Number Two

'I'd been trying to race bikes for a month with a broken neck.'

Everyone thought I was dead – except me because I wasn't thinking at all.

I lay unconscious in the gravel trap at Brands Hatch with my neck broken in two places, my spinal cord twisted into an 'S' shape and with a fragment of bone impregnated in the main nerve to my left arm. It was one of the most horrendous-looking crashes anyone had ever witnessed – and there were more than 100,000 people at the race that day. Even the national newspapers hailed it as the worst crash ever seen on TV.

World Superbike riders Neil Hodgson, Colin Edwards and Noriyuki Haga all got tangled up at about 120mph going into the fearsome Paddock Hill bend at Brands Hatch during the year 2000 WSB meeting. Neil had clipped the kerb because he couldn't see where he was going as all the other riders were so tightly bunched. His bike bounced back onto the track and started a chain reaction and I got caught up in the mêlée as Haga rammed my back wheel and Edwards took my front wheel away. The result was total carnage: there were bikes and riders tumbling everywhere, bits and pieces flying off the machinery and scything through the air and sparks showering down the track as metal collided with tarmac.

As my bike was rammed, I was thrown 15 feet in the air and started cartwheeling towards the gravel trap. My bike was spinning end over end and it slammed into my head twice – all 350lb of it – sending me tumbling even more spectacularly. It's a good job it did too because, ironically, that's probably what saved my life. The first smack it gave me knocked me out so I was unconscious as I tumbled and that meant my body was limp and relaxed. Had I been conscious and tensed up, I would probably have done even more damage to myself.

After doing four full-body cartwheels, I landed square on the top of my head with my feet pointing straight up in the air, as if I'd been planted in the ground by the celebrity gardener, Alan Titchmarsh. Then finally I tumbled over, came to a halt and slumped into the gravel, knocked out cold and lifeless as the dust began to settle and the bike finally came to a stop. The race was stopped immediately and the huge crowd that had been screaming and cheering just seconds before then, fell completely silent. Joey Dunlop had been killed in a race just one month previously and no one wanted to witness more tragedy at what should have been a fun day out. I don't know what the millions of armchair fans watching on TV around the world thought but what did annoy me afterwards was that it took such a horrific crash to get bike racing onto the main news. Usually the sport is never considered important enough to be mentioned on TV news bulletins unlike football, cricket, golf, Formula One or tennis. It was only when I had such a horrendous smash that almost every country in the world ran a story on it. What a way to get famous.

But if it weren't for the TV coverage, I wouldn't be able to describe the crash in detail because I can't remember it. The last thing I remember was feeling a thump when I was banking hard into Paddock Hill bend and that must have been when Haga hit me. Because the crash looked so bad and because I had landed on my head and wasn't moving, everyone who witnessed it presumed I was dead. My girlfriend Kelly, who was watching on TV back home, was in hysterics and couldn't get through to anyone in my team when she tried to call to find out if I was alive or dead. The Virgin Yamaha team wasn't taking calls because they were too busy trying to find out if they still had a rider. Kelly had to wait for about two hours before she got through to someone who told her I was OK. At first she didn't believe it and thought I must at least be in a coma, but someone finally convinced her that I was conscious and moving.

The first thing I remember through a foggy, dizzy haze was hearing a paramedic's voice shouting, 'there's a good vein, stick it in there,' as they immediately tried to stabilize me by hooking me up to an IV drip and an oxygen mask. Apart from that, everything was completely silent as the crowd looked on numbed and fearing the worst. There were paramedics swarming all over me and thankfully they knew to remove my helmet carefully with the aid of a neck brace because there was a risk of spinal injuries.

As I was stretchered off to the nearest hospital I started coming round a little and that's when I felt a pain in my chest and thought I might have broken my back. I was also getting a prickly feeling every time a medic touched me but it turned out that I was just covered in thousands of scratches from the gravel as I tumbled through it.

Anyone who thinks motorcycle racing is glamorous only needs to experience one big crash to realize it's not. The frequent injuries are bad enough to deal with but the undignified hospital procedures are just as bad. On this occasion, I was still feeling groggy when a doctor wearing rubber gloves approached me and that can mean only one thing. Sure enough, I jolted as he inserted a finger straight up my backside and had a prod around but at least he was kind enough to explain the theory he was putting into practice. Apparently, men have a kind of ultra-sensitive G-spot up there and if you hit the ceiling when the doctor touches it, you've got a broken back. I'd have thought most blokes would hit the ceiling anyway when a doctor shoves a finger up their arse, broken back or not but apparently I didn't flinch too violently so the prognosis was good even if the examination wasn't.

I was then x-rayed and pushed into a little cubicle

and left on my own for what seemed like an eternity as I still hadn't a clue what was happening to me. Coming round from concussion is not a nice experience and even though I'd been knocked out several times before, it doesn't get any easier because you're starting from scratch every time it happens as you've got no memories to draw upon.

I was really scared lying in there trying to piece my world together bit by bit. Where am I? What day is it? What year is it? The answer to every question was the same – I didn't know. I could only lie there like a newborn baby staring at the curtains round my bed, my brain completely devoid of any memory, any sense of belonging or any history; any sense of anything in fact. It really was like being born again – I didn't have a bloody clue what was going on.

Eventually, with a huge effort, I remembered I'd been at Brands Hatch but I still couldn't remember what year it was. I became convinced it was 1999 and only realized it was the year 2000 because I remembered which front suspension system I'd been using on the bike and that I'd been swapping between 1999 and 2000-spec forks that season. It's the most horrible, helpless feeling there is but for bike racers, it comes with the territory and you've just got to get on with it.

Some time later, my team boss, Rob McElnea, came in to see me and started asking me questions. As a former racer himself, he knew the routine for concussion as well as anyone and when I could tell him who I was, where I was and what year it was he reckoned I was all right and tried to get me to sign myself out.

The doctors had checked all the x-rays and said the only thing that concerned them was a cloudy area around the C5 and C6 vertebrae in my neck. I told them I'd had a prolapsed disc in 1995 at that very spot which seemed to explain the cloudy area. I hate hospitals and when I looked around and saw an old woman who had choked on a sandwich and another old girl who hadn't been able to shit for a month I thought, 'I hate these places – I need to get out of here.' So I signed myself out, even though the doctors wanted to keep me in overnight for observation, and I went back to the hotel that night. The following morning I drove my hire car to the airport and was back home on the Isle of Man a couple of hours after that.

When I saw a video of the crash on ITN news I realized how close to death or paralysis I had come. It looked much worse than triple world champion Wayne Rainey's crash at Misano in 1993 did and he's now wheelchair-bound for life because of that incident. Being paralysed or maimed scares me more than anything else in the world so I'd readily have chosen death over being stuck in a wheelchair. But then that's a choice we never get to make – fate decides it for us.

But I wasn't paralysed, I was just in pain all over. My head hit the inside of my helmet so hard that the mesh lining was imprinted on my forehead, and my forehead itself was so badly swollen that I looked like a Neanderthal. I had a black eye, my face was covered in cuts from where my helmet visor had come off allowing gravel to scratch my forehead and even my eyebrows were sore, although I can't think how that happened. I felt as if I'd been put through a full cycle in a washing machine. However everything seemed to be in working order and I figured I'd be fully fit again in a few days, so that, as far as I was concerned, was the end of my Brands Hatch crash. I couldn't have been more wrong.

Just four days later I set off for a round of the British Superbike championship at Knockhill in Scotland. Everyone in the paddock was amazed to see me on my feet and most people, I think, were glad to see me alive. I managed to qualify for the races but felt really weak and couldn't hold myself up on the bike properly. I figured I must have come back too early and since there were two weeks to recuperate before the next round at Cadwell Park, I decided to sit out the Knockhill meeting just to be on the safe side.

During those two weeks I had some physiotherapy and tried to lift some light weights but I still felt really weak down my left hand side. Then a really peculiar thing started to happen – I started walking into doors. I would put my left hand out to push open a door but my arm just buckled under the slightest strain so I'd end up slamming my face into the door. I wasn't in any pain (apart from the fact that I kept banging my nose), but I just had no strength or feeling in my left arm. It was weird.

Anyway, I went to Cadwell as planned but in the first few laps of practice it was apparent that something wasn't right. When you brake for a corner on a motorcycle you lift your body up out of the racing crouch to act as a windbreak which helps slow you down. This involves locking your arms against the handlebars as you lift up but every time I tried it I almost fell off the left-hand side of the bike. My left arm was just folding under pressure and it was way too dangerous to continue. I tried taking the strain on my knees against the fuel tank or with just my right arm on the bar but nothing seemed to work, so after six laps I pulled into the pits.

Everyone asked me what was wrong and I said I had no idea. I wasn't in pain, I just couldn't ride the bloody bike. Rob McElnea got really mad because he thought I was cracking up. I've been blamed a lot over the years for being fragile or temperamental when it comes to racing a bike because my results have not always been consistent and Rob probably thought that I just couldn't be bothered to ride or that I'd lost my bottle for some reason.

You've got to realize that in motorcycle sport, it's very common for riders to compete with freshly broken bones, torn ligaments or any other number of painful injuries. A trackside doctor is always on hand to administer painkilling injections to numb the pain for the duration of the race if required and riders often have special lightweight casts made to hold broken bones in place while they race. Basically, they will try anything just to go out and score some points so for me to explain that I was not in pain but just couldn't ride the bike must have sounded a bit odd to say the least.

Anyway, there was no way I could race but I hung

around Cadwell anyway and at one point bumped into a neurosurgeon I knew called Ian Sabin. He was a bike-racing fan and came to meetings when time permitted. I explained my problem so he carried out a few tests in the mobile clinic that attends all race meetings. He asked me to push against his hands as he held them out and I nearly pushed him over with my right hand but couldn't apply any pressure at all with my left hand. After another couple of simple tests he told me I had nerve damage and needed to get an MRI scan as soon as possible.

I went to London for a scan and had to pay the £600 fee out of my own pocket but it was the best £600 I've ever spent as it probably saved my life (and I eventually claimed it back through my insurance anyway). Ian looked at the results and I could immediately tell he was worried. He didn't tell me what he saw at that point but called another department and told them I needed an ECG test immediately. It was only then that he turned to me and said, 'Steven, you have a broken neck. What's more, you have been walking around and trying to race bikes for the last four weeks with a broken neck.'

Fuck! I couldn't believe what I was hearing. How could I possibly have a broken neck and not notice? How did the hospital not diagnose it straight after the race? How do you fix a broken neck? Would I be able to ride again? All of these thoughts were rushing through my head as Ian explained that the C5 and C6 vertebra in my neck were broken and badly crushed as well. As a result of that my spinal column was twisted into an 'S' shape and to further complicate matters, a piece of sheared bone was chafing against the main nerve which controlled my left arm and was threatening to cut through it. No wonder I had no strength in it.

Ian said that I'd been incredibly lucky over the previous month because my head was, quite literally, hanging on by a bunch of fibres with no support from my spine. If I'd been slapped in the face or had knocked my head in any way, then that would have been the end of it – I'd have been dead, or even worse in my book, paralysed from the neck down. I thought back to all the daft things I'd done over the last month like going out on the piss when I could easily have fallen over. If I'd fallen off the bike at Knockhill or Cadwell, even if I'd slept on my neck in a funny position the results could have been catastrophic for me. The odds of not damaging the injury further in that month were incredible but somehow I'd beaten them. You could call it luck but I prefer to think of it as destiny: it simply wasn't my time to die.

During the ECG test, they stuck needles in almost every muscle of my body and eventually found out that it was the nerve to my tricep muscle, in the rear of my left arm that had the most damage. It was deteriorating more with every passing day as the stray piece of bone gradually sawed its way through, and so I was scheduled for an operation as soon as possible.

Whilst I waited for the operation, I re-evaluated my entire life. I thought about everything I had done, pondered on everything I still wanted to do, and gradually realized how amazingly lucky I was to be getting a second chance at life when by all accounts, I should have been dead. I never once thought of quitting racing.

I'd never really believed there was a God and the crash didn't change my mind. If there was a God, why would he have allowed my father to die in my arms when I was just 17? Why would he have allowed my kid brother to be killed racing a bike when he was only 19? Why, after my mother had lost her husband and son within three years of each other, would he then pair her off with an abusive second husband who battered her regularly? Why would he have allowed a good friend of mine to be beaten to death outside a chip shop because he refused to give his chicken and chips to a gang of thugs? No, I was pretty sure God didn't exist or if He did, I didn't like His way of doing things.

I also thought of how many of my friends and racing colleagues had been killed in racing accidents over the years while my own life had been spared so miraculously. The list makes for grim and depressive reading: names such as Joey Dunlop, Phil Mellor, Steve Henshaw, Ray Swann, Kenny Irons, Sam McClements, Simon Beck, Lee Pullan, Colin Gable, Gene McDonnell, Mark Farmer, Robert Holden, Klaus Klein, Donny Robinson, Neil Robinson, Steve Ward and Mick Lofthouse. I could go on but it's not something I like to dwell on. We're all going to die if we live long enough and I became more hardened to death than most people after losing my father and brother, so racing deaths never bothered me as much as they might have done.

But each and every one of those riders chose to dedicate his life to the sport of motorcycle racing because he loved it. It's a sport that delivers thrills like no other but also one that punishes mistakes more harshly and more violently than any other. The risks are multiplied 10-fold when a rider also decides to race on closed public road tracks like the notorious Isle of Man TT. It is undoubtedly the most dangerous racing event in the world, but it's also the event where I made my name and where I enjoyed so many great victories.

Since its inception in 1907, over 170 riders have been killed at the TT and the list is added to almost every year. Some years, as many as five riders are killed in the two-week event. Yet I won there 11 times at speeds which no one had ever witnessed before. Racing between walls and houses at over 190mph and averaging over 120mph for a lap was an awesome rush even if it was highly dangerous. But I cheated death on the world's most unforgiving racetrack for 10 years and was never even hurt once while racing there. Ironically, it was a so-called 'safe', purpose-built short circuit that nearly claimed my life and almost left my mother with no sons at all.

I pondered on all these things as I awaited my operation and repeatedly questioned why I still wanted to race motorbikes more than anything else in my life. It certainly wasn't for the financial rewards since I haven't made any serious money from racing even though I've raced for more than 20 years. The truth is that when I retire I'll have to get a normal job like everybody else because I have no savings worth talking about. Some racers, like my former team-mate, Carl Fogarty, have become millionaires from the sport but I've been financially naive throughout my career and consequently never got the rewards I feel I deserve.

Having said that, racing at least gives me some sort of wage to live on from day to day, so I suppose money was one of the reasons I had to get back on a bike again. After all, I have two small sons to support with no other obvious means of earning cash to feed and clothe them. But more than anything I wanted to get back on a bike again because I desperately wanted to win the British Superbike championship – the toughest domestic race series in the world.

Throughout my career people have always thought I could only win on dangerous street circuits and couldn't adapt my style to the short sprint, purpose-built tracks, which require a different and more aggressive riding style. Even when I won the 250cc British championship in 1990 on short circuits people said I just got lucky, so the 'road racer' tag still weighed heavily round my neck.

In 1995 I won the British Superbike series but this time pundits said it was only because my arch-rival Jamie Whitham developed cancer midway through the season. It seemed as if nothing I did was enough to convince people that I was a world class short-circuit rider who could hold his own against the best in the world.

After winning that title in '95 I had seven years of bad luck in the BSB series. Two of my teams folded mid-season through lack of funds, two other teams sacked me for 'under performing' and I didn't complete three seasons because of injury. So, more than anything, I wanted to come back from my injuries this time and win the British title so convincingly that no one could ever have any more doubts about my ability on a motorcycle.

I don't mind admitting that I was absolutely shitting myself going into that operation. Motorcycle racing may be dangerous but at least I was always the one in control: I could back off the throttle or slam on the brakes if things got too hot or I could even pull off the track and quit if I was totally unhappy about something. There was at least some sense of being in charge even if it was only a delusion. But being knocked out and having someone, however well qualified, operating on your spine? That's really scary.

Lower spine operations are quite common and generally successful but the neck is a different matter. From the chest upwards, it's like a bloody telephone exchange inside your body with all those nerves crisscrossing each other and that's where things can go wrong. As I've said, my biggest fear is being paralysed so if the surgeons were going to mess up, I'd rather they just put me to sleep for good.

You'd think that for an operation on your neck, the surgeons would go in from the back, but in my case at least, they didn't. Instead, they cut open my throat, pushed my windpipe aside and went to work from there. They picked out all the shattered pieces of bone and generally cleaned up the mess, then they cut open my hip and chipped a disc of bone from my pelvis to graft into my neck. I swear they must have used a bloody sledgehammer to chip that bone off because the pain in my pelvis when I woke up was like nothing on earth and I've had my share of serious injuries so I'm well accustomed to pain.

As you'd expect, I was also pretty groggy when I woke up and I remember wondering why the fuck there was a red Christmas tree bulb hanging out of my pelvis and one hanging out of my neck too. As I came a bit more to my senses I realized they were blood drains – little suction pumps that suck out any surplus blood so it doesn't start congealing. My neck and throat felt OK but that bloody hip was unbelievable and when Ian wanted me on my feet the morning after the operation I was horrified. Man that hurt.

Anyway, normally that procedure would have been enough and any other patient would be told to take it easy for a while until the bone healed itself. But because my surgeon knew I wanted to go racing again as soon as possible, he strengthened my neck by screwing in a titanium plate which I still have in there – and always will have as a matter of fact.

A CT scan showed the operation had gone well and my neck was stable and I was on my way home two days later, but I'd been told there was no guarantee that I'd ever get any feeling or strength back in my left arm. Ian said it might return in six weeks, six months, one year or perhaps never at all. I had almost torn that nerve clean out of the spinal column as my body was twisted in the crash and no one could tell if my arm would ever be anything more than the relatively lifeless object that was dangling by my side. I was at nature's mercy.

Every day for weeks – even though I don't believe in God – I prayed for some feeling to come back, but every day for weeks it didn't. I tried to build up strength in it but could only lift light weights and I was starting to get really depressed thinking my career was over and that I was going to be left with a useless arm. I couldn't even try to set up a deal for the following season because I didn't know if I'd be able to ride a bike or not.

Then one day, about two months after the crash, it started happening. I felt a slight sensation on the back of my hand and then in my index finger. It wasn't much but it was definitely something. I thought, 'Yes! Here we go, I'm back in business.' I felt totally elated but not as elated as I was when, near Christmas time, I was finally able to lock my left arm out fully. That was the best Christmas present I'd had since my first son was born on Christmas Day in 1997. I was over the moon.

It was game on after that and I started training slowly and gently to rebuild some muscle in my wasted arm. That was day number one of life number two as far as I was concerned and I never stopped thinking about racing after that. There were still some months until the start of the new season so I had time to try and organize a ride for the year, even though I'd burned my bridges with most teams over the last few years. But I didn't care – I'd been given a second chance at life and I wasn't about to waste it. Somehow I would find a bike to race even if it meant remortgaging my house and buying one myself. The way I saw it, I had nothing to lose because I should have been dead anyway.

Steve Hislop was back – and he was going to win the British Superbike championship come hell or high water.

Shooting Crows

**'My real name's actually Robert Hislop but my
dad made a mistake when he registered me.'**

The Isle of Man TT is a totally unique event and probably attracts more controversy than any other sporting
fixture on the calendar.

It's held on the world famous 'Mountain' circuit
that runs over 37.74 miles of everyday public roads
on the Isle of Man. The roads are, naturally, closed for
the races but they're still lined with hazards such as
houses, walls, lamp-posts, hedges and everything else
you would expect to find on normal country roads.

Because of the dangers and the number of competitors who have been killed there, the event lost its
world championship status in 1976 when top riders
like Barry Sheene, Phil Read and Giacomo Agostini
refused to race there any longer. When you consider
that the current, fastest *average* lap speed is held by
David Jefferies at 127.29mph and bikes have been
speed-trapped at 194mph between brick walls, it's
easy to understand the dangers of the place, as there's

no run-off space when things go wrong. But the thrill of riding there is unique and that's what keeps so many riders coming back year after year.

Riders don't all start together at the TT – they set off singly at 10-second intervals in a bid to improve safety although mass starts have occurred in the past. That means the competitors are racing against the clock and the longest races last for six laps which equates to 226 miles and about two hours in the saddle at very high speeds and on very bumpy roads. It's an endurance test as much as anything else and you can't afford to lose concentration for a split second or you are quite literally taking your own life in your hands. It is an event like no other on earth.

The TT (which stands for Tourist Trophy) fortnight is traditionally held in the last week of May and the first week of June and the Manx Grand Prix is traditionally held on the same course in September. The latter event is purely amateur with no prize money and it exists as a way for riders to learn the daunting 37.74 mile course before tackling the TT proper. The name should not be confused with the world championship Moto Grand Prix series because the two have nothing in common.

Both the Manx Grand Prix and the TT races have played a huge part in my life, which is why I'm describing them in detail now. Without them I simply wouldn't be where I am today, or even writing this book, and a basic understanding of the nature of both events is crucial to understanding my later career.

I first visited the Manx GP as a child, then later on

spent 10 years racing on the Mountain course, both at the Manx and the TT. I grew to love the Isle of Man so much over the years that I moved there in 1991 and it's where I still live to this day.

It was my father Alexander, or 'Sandy' as he was known, who got me interested in the TT and the Manx GP in the first place as he raced at the Manx back in the 1950s. I went on to have incredible success at the TT and that's really where I made my name in the world of motorcycling. But believe it or not, the Steve Hislop who won 11 TT races (only two men in history have won more) isn't actually called Steve at all thanks to one of the daftest blunders anyone's dad ever made.

I may be known as Steve Hislop throughout the bike-racing world but on every piece of documentation that proves who I am, the name given is actually Robert. I still don't know exactly how it happened but it was definitely my dad's doing. Both he and my mum, Margaret, had decided on calling me Steven Robert Hislop and that's the name I was christened under, but my dad messed up big time. For reasons known only to him, he registered me as Robert Steven Hislop and to this day even my passport carries that name.

Robert was my grandfather's name, but he died when he was just 30 after he fell from the attic in his dad's blacksmith's workshop. His was the first in a series of tragic early deaths in my family.

I was born at 7.55pm on 11 January 1962 at the Haig Maternity Hospital in Hawick in the Scottish Borders.

But although I was born in a Hawick hospital, I'm not actually from the town itself despite what all those race programmes, TV commentators and magazine articles have said over the years. I'm actually from the little village of Chesters in a parish called Southdean, a few miles south east of Hawick. My mum was only 16 when she had me, while my dad was a good bit older at 26 – a bit of a cradle snatcher was the old boy!

Money was tight so we all lived with my widowed granny for the first few months of my life. Mum worked in the knitwear mills; knitwear is a big trade in the Borders and my dad was a joiner who worked for a small country joinery firm in Chesters village before eventually buying the business when the owner died.

My younger brother, Garry Alexander Hislop, was born in the same hospital as me on 28 July 1963, just 17 months after I was and we were very close right from the start. I loved having a brother.

Dad loved his bikes and was very friendly with the late, great Bob McIntyre, another Scottish bike racer and the first man ever to lap the Isle of Man TT course at 100mph. Dad raced between 1956 and 1961 on a BSA Gold Star and a 350cc Manx Norton. He travelled to all the little Scottish courses that don't exist any more, such as Charter Hall, Errol, Crimond and Beveridge Park, including some circuits in the north of England such as Silloth – a track which would later have tragic consequences for my family.

He was a pretty handy racer in the Scottish championships but never really had the money to do it properly. He used to ride to meetings on his bike with a racing exhaust strapped to his back, fit it to the bike for the race then change back to the standard one and ride home again! That was proper clubman's racing. As I mentioned earlier, my dad also raced at the Manx Grand Prix a few times usually finishing midfield but when mum became pregnant with me he packed in the racing game to support the family.

As a kid, I went to Hobkirk primary school. I remember being absolutely shit-scared, waiting for the bus on my first day of school because I was a very shy child and hadn't mixed much with other kids since most of the time I just played with my little brother. Shyness is something I have mostly grown out of now but it was definitely a problem for me in the early days of my career.

I can't remember much about primary school except that I always seemed to be sticking up for Garry in fights, particularly with a kid called Magoo who was always picking on him. My other outstanding memory of primary school was of Mr Thompson, the head teacher, who had a wooden leg, though I never found out why. Instead of giving us the belt when we were bad, he pulled our hair repeatedly! I clearly remember him telling me off and yanking the tuft of hair at the front of my head in time with his rantings. No wonder I've got no bloody hair left!

My secondary school was Jedburgh Grammar, but I was never interested in going there because I was a real out-door type, thanks to my dad's uncles, Jim and John Wallace, having a farm. Almost every weekend I would cycle down to that farm and have the time of my life. I fed the sheep and the cows, picked the turnips and generally mucked in with the chores, then after that it was back to the house for a big farm breakfast and in the afternoons John and I would go shooting.

At that point, all I wanted to be when I grew up was a gamekeeper. I was like a little old man with my deerstalker hat with the 'Deputy Dawg' flap-down ear covers and a bloody big shotgun cocked over my arm. I used to feed up all the birds and ducks and make little hideouts round the ponds then come the shooting season I blew the hell out of everything that could fly – and some things that couldn't.

I know that sounds cruel now but that was the norm in the country, especially back then, and boys will be boys after all. Having said that, I was a bit of a nasty little fucker when it came to things like that. I shot baby crows that had left the nest with my .22 rifle and kept the shotgun for the bigger birds and the nests themselves. I'm not particularly proud of it now but as I said before, it felt normal at the time.

On Sunday evenings I would cycle home again as late as I could get away with and dreaded going back to school the next day. I had pushbikes from a very early age but they were always hand-me-downs and were far too big for me. I never had any stabilizers either so I had lots of crashes because I was too small to reach the ground. My folks would hold on to me to get me going then seconds after they let me go there would be a big crashing noise, a yelp and a puff of dust as I hit the deck again. But I loved two-wheelers from the start, even when they were too big for me.

The first time I ever got a new bike was when my nana bought Garry and I brand new Raleigh Choppers for Christmas but they were just as dangerous as the too-big hand-me-downs. Choppers may have looked cool but they certainly weren't designed for riding – they were bloody lethal. Garry once smashed his face to hell one night when he crashed cycling down a hill and he squealed in pain all the way home – the poor little bugger. We used to get into high-speed wobbles because the front wheels were so small and the high bars provided so much leverage that they made the effect worse.

Even back then we pretended we were riding motorbikes and like most kids at the time, we gripped playing cards onto the fork legs with clothes pegs so they ran through the spokes and made a noise like a motorbike. But showing an early aptitude for setting up machinery, I eventually found that cut-up bottles of washing-up liquid lasted longer than playing cards and made a better noise too!

Before we even had pushbikes, my mum says that Garry and I would sit in the house and pretend to be bike racers. We would be at opposite ends of the sofa over the armrests in a racing crouch, our little legs dangling over the side, and cushions under our chests acting as petrol tanks.

Apparently we fought over which racer we were pretending to be too and it was always Jimmie Guthrie or Geordie Buchan. Jimmie Guthrie was Hawick's most famous son and one of the greatest names in pre-war motorcycle racing. He was born in 1897 and went on to win six Isle of Man TTs and was European champion three times when that title was the equivalent of today's world championships. His admirers included none other than a certain Adolf Hitler who on one occasion even presented him with a trophy!

Jimmie was killed in a 500cc race at the Sachsenring in Germany in 1937 at 40 years of age and there's still a statue of him in Hawick, as well as the famous Guthrie's memorial on the TT course. Like I said before, Garry and I would argue over who was going to be Jimmy Guthrie and who was going to be Geordie Buchan, who was the Scottish champion at the time and also a friend of my dad. So in a sense, my first ever race was on a sofa and I think it finished in a dead heat with Garry!

Rugby is the big sport in the Scottish Borders and although I played it at school, I was never a big fan. In fact, I never liked football or tennis either and as for cricket – what the fuck is that all about? I'll never understand the fascination with that game. It's just grown men playing bloody rounders if you ask me. I was more into hunting and shooting things. My old Uncle John also taught me the art of fly fishing and I loved that too. I don't do it any more but I suppose I'll have to relearn it now to teach my own kids, Connor and Aaron.

However, I hope they never have to go through the experience I once had when I went sea fishing with my dad and Garry. Dad owned a little boat that we used to tow to the coast for a spot of line-and-rod fishing. On one occasion we took it to the Isle of Whithorn in Galloway and were anchored over some rocks on the Solway Firth doing a spot of rod fishing. It was a lovely hot, calm day so we didn't have any life jackets on and everything was just perfect, the sun on our backs and the water lapping gently at the hull of the boat. But all of a sudden the peace was shattered by my dad screaming, 'Get your bloody life jackets on boys, NOW! And get your rods in. QUICKLY.' I turned to see what the hell could be causing all this panic and was startled to spot a huge dorsal fin heading directly for the boat. Bloody hell, I shat myself; it was a huge basking shark, more than twice the size of the boat (which was 16 feet long) and it was coming straight for us!

Although I didn't know it then, basking sharks are harmless plankton feeders but they look just like great white sharks and are much, much bigger, growing to well over 30 feet. That's pretty damned big when you're a scrawny little four-foot kid. This all happened just two years before the movie *Jaws* came out and I'm pretty glad I hadn't seen that film beforehand because I'd probably have been even more terrified and I was scared enough as it was. The shark went under the boat and I remember seeing its head emerging on the other side before its tail had even gone under – that's how big it was. It just continued swimming away and that's the last we saw of it, but it was a pretty scary experience – even though it was good to brag about later.

Garry and I were very close and I suppose we

had to be really because there were very few other kids to play with. Obviously, we fought a bit as all boys do but we were the best of pals most of the time. We built tree houses and hammocks, messed about in the woods and by the rivers and had a real boys' own childhood. We did used to pal around with a guy called David Cook, or 'Cookie' as we called him, who went on to become a 250cc Scottish bike racing champion, but he was about the only other kid we were close to.

Way before we ever got motorbikes, Cookie, Garry and I used to hone our racing skills in 45-litre oil drums. Two of us would squeeze into a drum and the third person would push it down a massive hill. It was brilliant fun to be in the drum but just as much of a laugh watching the other two getting beaten up as they bounced and rattled their way downhill, bones clattering all the way. Eventually we came up with a new addition to the game – a tractor tyre! This thing was bigger than all three of us but we managed to wheel it up the hill then I'd spend ages trying to squeeze my way inside it as if I was an inner tube. Once I was in, the lads would give me a mighty shove and off I went, bouncing and bouncing for what seemed like ages as the heavy tyre picked up speed on its way down the hill. That bit was all right – it was the slowing down followed by the inevitable crash that caused the many injuries. I'd get thrown out at the end as the momentum died out and I was usually really dizzy and disorientated from being spun round like a hamster in a wheel, so invariably I fell on my backside as soon as I tried to stand up.

One time I actually fell out of the tyre while it was still bouncing down the hill at speed and I crashed face first into a grassy knoll and bust my nose. It was bleeding and swollen and in a hell of a mess. I don't know if it was actually broken, but to this day I've still got a kink in my nose and it was all because of that bloody tractor tyre.

As kids, our other passion was for bogeys, or fun karts, as people call them now. You know the type, a wooden base with four pram wheels and a rope for steering. We got really good at building them and even made one with a cab once. There was a steep downhill corner in the field next to our house which was good for learning to slide the bogeys on but we decided a bit of mud would help make it even slippier. I don't know why we didn't just soak it with water but instead we had the bright idea of pissing on that corner for all we were worth to make it muddy so we could get better slides! If we didn't need to pee, we'd simply drink bottles and bottles of juice until we did – the more piss the better as far as we were concerned. We would eventually get the corner so wet that we had out of control slides and Garry once had a huge crash and ended up lying in that huge puddle of piss with several broken fingers.

It was a happy time for Garry and I, and it may have seemed idealistic at the time but in later years I realized the more negative effects my upbringing had on me. Because I was so isolated, I was very shy with other people. I still am today, to a certain extent, so I'm trying to encourage my kids to be confident and to mix freely with people so that they're better equipped to deal with the big bad world than I was. Even now, I hate calling travel agents and bank managers or dealing with any 'official' phone calls like that, so if I can, I ask someone else to do it for me! I know that sounds pathetic, but it's just the way I am.

There was another couple of kids, called Alistair and Norman Glendinning, with whom Garry and I sometimes played. They lived on a nearby farm called Doorpool. At the time, we were renting a cottage within the farm grounds which cost seven shillings a week (35 pence in today's money), if my mum agreed to top up the water trough for the cows every day, which she did.

Once I remember having a big argument with Alistair Glendinning and I ended up throwing a garden rake at him. It split his face open and cut his head – he was in a right mess. I got a terrible bollocking for that but a few days later we were all playing happily together again. Kids don't hold grudges, shame adults aren't the same.

When I was nine years old, in 1973, my dad, as a former competitor, was invited to the Golden Jubilee of the Manx Grand Prix. When he got there he met up with Jim Oliver who owned Thomas B. Oliver's garage in Denholm, just a few miles from where we lived. Jim was partly sponsoring a rider called Wullie Simson, who also lived near our home and my dad got to know him on that trip. It turned out that Wullie was a joiner like my dad but he'd quit his job when his boss wouldn't give him time off to go to the Manx! My dad was getting a lot of work in so he offered Wullie a job, which was gladly accepted. Garry and I helped out at my dad's workshop for pocket money and we liked Wullie straight away when he started there and we were always asking him about the racing.

Some two weeks after Wullie started his job at the workshop, my dad asked Garry and I if we'd like to go and watch some bike racing at Silloth, an airfield circuit just south of Carlisle. Too right we did! We were so excited at the prospect that we could hardly sleep. When Garry and I had been about five or six years old, we went with our nana and papa to stay in a caravan at Silloth. I remember hearing motorbikes howling away in the background and my grandma explained it was the bike racing over on the airfield. I ranted and begged her for so long to take us to see them that the poor woman ended up trudging with us for about six miles on the round trip to the airfield just so we could watch the bikes. There was a big delay in the racing because a rider was killed and my nana wanted to take Garry and I away from the track at that point, but I was having none of it. Apparently, I refused to leave the circuit until I'd seen the last bike in the last race go past. I obviously loved bike racing even way back then. That must have been in the late 1960s.

But I was 11 and old enough to really appreciate it properly by the time dad took me back to Silloth to watch another race and my most vivid memory of that meeting is of a guy in purple leathers, because everyone else was wearing black. Every lap he came out of the hairpin and pulled a big wheelie and I thought he was amazing. He was called Steve Machin and I'm now very friendly with his brother Jack though sadly later, Steve himself was killed on a race bike.

It was great to watch my dad's mate Wullie Simson racing and he must have enjoyed our support because soon after that race, he turned up at our house in his van and pulled out a Honda ST50. It must have been an MOT failure or something because the engine was in pieces but my dad soon put it back together, got it fired up and that was it. From that moment on, Garry and I spent every spare moment riding that bike in the field surrounding the house. My motorcycling career had begun.

The Burger Van Queue

'If I hadn't gone for a burger I wouldn't have won that first TT.'

As if my mum hadn't had enough to cope with in losing her husband and son I found out she had more problems towards the end of 1986 in the form of an abusive second husband.

Apparently my stepdad had been hitting her for some time but mum had never said anything to me about it so I was completely in the dark until one night when I came home early from a race meeting in England. I was supposed to be racing at Donington one Sunday but my gearbox blew up so I drove home early on the Saturday night and got to the pub at about 1.30am. I noticed the lights were still on as I parked the van, went inside and then I heard a commotion. I could hear mum screaming at Jim as I walked through the door and was horrified to see her cowering in a corner while Jim stood over her brandishing a pool cue.

Now I'm only a 10-stone weakling but I have one

hell of a temper, and when I'm in a rage I don't even think about the consequences of what I'm doing and no one was going to beat up my mum as long as I was still breathing. I ran straight towards that bastard screaming, 'What the fuck's going on here?' He yelled back at me saying I was a, 'useless waste of space', as he started moving towards me. That piece of shit was ex-army and he was about six feet tall, but I lunged out and punched him on the chin so hard he went flying over the bar and landed in a heap amongst a pile of broken bottles. The combined speed of us running towards each other had been enough to launch him over the bar and he flew over it John Wayne-style. I couldn't believe my mum had been putting up with this after all she'd had to deal with.

Mum stayed with Jim for a while after that but it turned out he was still being abusive and I had another run-in with him about a year later when he came back from the golf club on one occasion, all pissed-up and aggressive. I told him to shut up or go to bed and he started telling me I was a waste of space again and went to have another go at me, so I hit back and this time broke his nose. Jim went to the police and wanted them to arrest me. The local papers even ran a story on the whole thing but the police treated it as a domestic incident and it all blew over without any action being taken against me. I ended up leaving the house after that and went to live with Jim Oliver and his wife Rae. I'd finally had enough of that bastard and my mum decided she had too so she finally left him for good, which was the best move she ever made. I've never seen that guy again since I broke his nose and that's just fine by me. I hope it stays that way.

I stayed with Jim and Rae until I found a place to rent just across the road from Jim's garage and my mum moved in with me too, but I nearly burned the place down not long after we'd moved in! The house was a bit damp and dingy so on one particularly cold night I lit a big fire with wood, old boots and anything else I could find. I then went over the road to see Jim and soon afterwards someone phoned to say my house was on fire. I ran back across the road and sure enough, my mum's bedroom was well on its way to being burned out. She had a boarded-up fireplace in there and my huge fire downstairs had set light to the board which had then fallen onto the floor and started setting everything else alight. But what really got it going was a doll mum had had since childhood, which was one of her most prized possessions. It was completely melted by the time I managed to put the fire out but after all my mum had been through lately, losing a doll didn't seem that important.

Despite all the trials and traumas of my home life, I tried to focus my attentions on the 1987 season. I couldn't wait to go racing again and as it turned out, that year proved to be a real watershed for me, when a lifetime's ambition came true and I finally put the Hislop name in the TT history books.

Everyone kept telling me that to set yourself up properly for the TT, you had to race at the North West 200 in Northern Ireland, so in 1987 I decided to give it a go. It's another pure roads course set on nine miles of public roads that link Portrush, Portstewart and Coleraine in County Antrim and it's a very, very fast circuit. Because the event is held in May, just a couple of weeks before the TT, it's an ideal way to set up your bikes and get honed back into pure road racing.

I had taken a step backwards at the start of 1987 because Marshall Lauder Knitwear folded and I was left with no backing once again. I resprayed my bike plain black and red and the only logos on it were for chains and sprockets, the usual small time product support that most racers get. I was even still buying my own leathers and helmets at that point.

The plan for the year was to race in the Super II championship in England as well as competing in the major road races which were, as always, the North West 200, the TT and the Ulster Grand Prix. I had really enjoyed the Ulster in 1986 so I was pretty sure I'd like the North West race as well.

I set off in my new van on my own, because my mates couldn't get time off work, and caught the ferry from Stranraer to Larne. I had never seen the course before so as soon as I found out where it was, I checked into a little B&B for the first night to enjoy a few home comforts before roughing it in the paddock again. I then set off to do a couple of laps in the van.

I was also taken round on the newcomers' bus which was a good idea but that was all I did before practice began. As I was setting up in the paddock for practice I met another guy who became a great friend over the years – Dave Leach. Dave was a great pure roads racer but he had a terrible accident at the

Tandragee road races in Ireland in 1992, when he was thrown from his bike and straddled a tree at extremely high speed. He literally slammed into the tree trunk with one leg either side of it and his injuries, as you can imagine, were horrendous. It took Dave years to recover from that and he still walks with a limp but he eventually made a comeback to racing, albeit as a shadow of his former self, before retiring for good in 1997.

I got a good lesson in road racing from Ian Newton and Irishman Gary Cowan (who was later paralysed in a racing accident at Daytona) during practice for the North West. I was right behind them on the run into the Ballysalla Roundabout where there's a hard shoulder at the side of the road. I had only been going out as far as the white line and not using the shoulder at all but those guys were using every inch of it, right into the gutter. They were riding the roads as if they were on a short circuit and it taught me to up my pace and use every inch of the track from then on. It's no longer any good riding at 80 per cent of the roads if you want to win – you have to ride flat out.

I was only entered on my 350 Yamaha and I had a great race with my hero, Joey Dunlop, for the first time. We were only battling for sixth and seventh but it was still awesome racing with the guy who had inspired me to race on the roads in the first place back in 1983. When the race was over and Joey had beaten me by just a wheel's length (I was still the first 350 machine home), he went to his manager, Davy Wood, and asked who I was. When Davy told him I was some Scottish bloke called Steve Hislop, Joey simply said, 'He'll win a TT one day, that boy.'

Joey was a god to me at that point so that was a real compliment but, unfortunately, it wasn't until years later that Davy Wood actually told me Joey had said that – I would have been really chuffed if I'd known at the time. I still hadn't met Joey at that point and it wasn't until I was at Honda UK's headquarters in 1988 that I met him for the first time. He was a man of very few words; he wasn't rude, he just didn't have much to say. As a Scot, I could always understand his broad Irish accent with no problem – although I know a lot of people couldn't – but there was never much to understand as he hardly ever spoke.

After the North West 200 it was time to think about the TT again. Once more I had Wullie Simson and Dave Croy helping me out and I was entered in the Formula Two and Junior races on the 350 and the Production D event on a Yamaha TZR250 which I'd been using in the TZR Challenge on the mainland. I was flying in practice and was on lap record pace for the Formula Two class on the second day, posting a 110mph lap which got everyone talking about me. They knew I was going to be on the pace that year and so did I because my newly learned short-circuit aggression was really paying dividends round the Island.

The Junior race was delayed because of bad weather but when I did set off I was riding number 28 on my 350 Yamaha with an intermediate tyre on the front and a slick on the back, hoping the course would dry out. I needed to stop for fuel every two laps whereas the 250cc machines could last three laps before refuelling so I knew that was going to be a disadvantage. But I set off at a cracking pace and as the track dried out I kept getting faster and clocked a lap at 111.5mph on the second circuit. After the pit stops had all been sorted out I was leading on lap four by about two minutes and looking good for my first TT win. But the Hislop jinx that would later become famous in the Junior TT struck on the fifth, and penultimate, lap.

I'd had some ignition problems in practice but hoped everything would be okay for the race – it wasn't. At Ballaspur on the fifth lap, the bike started coughing and spluttering and I was forced to pull in at Glen Helen. My race was over and I was gutted. I'd been holding a two-minute lead over riders as good as Brian Reid, Eddie Laycock, Joey Dunlop and Carl Fogarty and yet it all came to nothing. Bollocks!

It was nothing I'd done wrong, it was just an electrical problem with the Hitachi ignition unit I was using. But at least I got my face on TV for the first time as I was interviewed for the official TT video as I sat on the grass banking miserable as hell. I went out that night and got absolutely bladdered with Ray Swann and Roger Hurst. Those two boys were good buddies and good racers but they were as mad as fish and their friendship was to end in tragedy in 1990. Roger was driving a car while he was very drunk and Ray was in the passenger seat when another vehicle collided with them. Because Roger was drunk, he got the blame.

Ray was killed in that accident and Roger was sent to prison for quite some time but it's something he'll have to live with for the rest of his life.

Anyway, when I came out of the boozer I did what every self-respecting drunk does and went for a burger. I joined the huge queue at the burger bar and got talking to another racer called Phil 'Mez' Mellor. He asked what had happened and when I told him the Hitachi ignition had packed in he asked me if it had been a new one. I said I couldn't afford a new one because they cost hundreds of pounds so mine had been a reconditioned one. Mez, in his comedy Yorkshire accent said, 'Reconditioned units are shite mate. Throw that ignition in t' middle o' Irish Sea and get a new 'un.'

When I repeated that I couldn't afford a new one another voice piped up from further back in the queue. It was a guy called Roger Keene who just happened to sell Hitachi ignition units. He said he'd sell me a new one for £150, which was really cheap, but I told him I still didn't have that kind of money. That's when *another* voice piped up in the queue and joined the conversation. This time it was a bike sponsor called Colin Aldridge who I'd heard of but never actually met. Having overheard my sob story, Colin and his friend stuck their hands in their pockets there and then, gave some money to Roger Keene and said, 'Get this boy a new ignition tomorrow.' I couldn't believe it! That was the best burger I ever decided to buy and it proved that fast food isn't always bad for you.

I got the ignition the next day, fitted it, and was all ready to go for the Formula Two race. Surely this time my luck would hold? I certainly remember hearing the pop group Wet, Wet, Wet singing *Wishing I was Lucky* on the radio just before the race and thinking 'I wish I could be fucking lucky this time around.'

Brian Reid was leading the race on the second lap when, ironically, his ignition packed up just as mine had in the Junior race. As soon as I knew he was out I thought, 'Yes, I'm in with a chance here,' then I set a new lap record at 112.1mph on the following lap and built up a 20-second lead over Graeme McGregor and Eddie Laycock. My lead was up to 40 seconds by the end of lap three but then Laycock upped the pace and started catching as I backed off a bit trying to make sure my bike would hold out to the finish this time.

I was getting signals all round the course telling me what was going on in the race but you have to be careful with those sometimes. Most riders have their own crew doing signals but you always get some from other people who just do it to try to be helpful. That's fine most of the time but those people can often get it wrong. Sometimes I'd see a 'Hizzy third' then a 'Hizzy fifteenth' on the same lap or something daft like that so I tended to go with the most consistent times and hoped they were right.

It wasn't until I was heading over the mountain for the last time that I started thinking, 'Yes, I can really do this.' Then I became really distracted by the thought of winning and started talking to the bike saying, 'Come on, come on, please keep going, don't let me down this time, girl,' just urging my little bike on. I always muttered away to myself on the Island, cursing mistakes and encouraging the bike to make it home. If there had been a microphone inside my helmet it would have made for some pretty entertaining listening on occasions.

I had a big scare at Cronk-ny-Mona just a few miles from home when my rear tyre let go and nearly highsided me at speed. But I managed to keep upright and flashed across the finish line on the Glencrutchery Road 17 seconds ahead of Eddie Laycock: I had won an Isle of Man TT race.

To explain what that win felt like is not really possible. My father had raced on that course, my brother had won a Manx GP on it and I had been trying to win there for five years. I had even been going to the Island since I was a kid and dreamed that one day I'd stand on the winner's rostrum And this wasn't the Manx GP either, it was the TT proper and I simply couldn't have been more elated – and relieved. If I hadn't got drunk and gone for a burger, I wouldn't have won that TT; it was all down to having a new ignition that lasted race distance.

To win in front of Wullie Simson and Dave Croy was great, too, but I remember feeling really sad because my dad couldn't be there to see me win that race. Strangely enough, I thought about my dad more than about Garry but that's probably because my dad had got me into the whole racing thing and I knew how proud he would have been. If Garry had been alive, he'd probably have been on that rostrum too.

When I got back to the Doric hotel that night there were flags and banners hanging everywhere and the atmosphere was just brilliant. We all stayed in there that night and had a wild time and I got totally lashed-up for the second time that week!

My next race was the Production D event for 250cc two-strokes and 400cc four-stroke machines and it turned out to be a real giggle for me. I started off four places behind Carl Fogarty on my little TZR 250 Yamaha and caught him pretty quickly so we were racing together on the roads even though I was in front of him on corrected time. That's when the fun started. Because they were production bikes, like the ones you could buy in a showroom, they had horns fitted so we were peeping at each other all the way round the course! I would be saying, 'Get the hell out of my way Foggy you ugly bastard. Peep, peep!' Then he'd stuff it up the inside of me and switch his indicators on as he peeled into the next corner It was like that throughout the race and we had a brilliant time on those little bikes because they felt really slow which is why we had time to mess around. The straights went on forever and we'd be looking over at each other making faces or flipping the bird just to pass the time until the next corner.

It was great going back home after that first TT win as there was so much interest and support from the local people. All the newspapers ran stories and there was even a reception held for me in Denholm Town Hall, which was fantastic. After a few days I also started receiving some interest from the major manufacturers and that was what I really wanted. Andy Smith from Yamaha was the first to make contact when he called me at work. He said he'd be keen to give me some production bikes for the following year's TT and asked me to keep in touch.

The next call I got was from Mick Grant (a seven times TT winner himself) at Suzuki who also congratulated me and asked about my plans for 1988. Again, he offered me production bikes for the TT and asked me to stay in touch. But then came the big one. To me, Honda were the top dogs so when Bob McMillan called, I thought, 'Fuckin' hell, now we're talking.' Bob said he'd been watching me and liked my riding so he too offered me production bikes for the 1988 TT and I said I'd think about it.

The reason all the firms offered me production bikes as opposed to full race bikes is because they're a much cheaper way of getting results and there's less commitment required as far as preparing them goes. You can try out a rider on a relatively cheap production bike and if it doesn't work out there's not much lost. Putting a relatively new name on a precious and rare factory Superbike is a different matter. Anyway, Honda had the factory bikes covered with Joey Dunlop at that time, so there was even less chance of me being offered one.

I was flattered to have Honda's attention but still wasn't sure whose offer to accept; Yamaha had some good production bikes going at the time and I had always been a bit of a Yamaha man so I was quite happy to stay on Yams – until I saw Honda's RC30. That bike was getting lots of coverage in the press and it was hyped up to be the greatest road-going sports bike ever. To this day, I still think it is, as far as being revolutionary is concerned. To me, no bike has moved the game on as much as the RC30 did when it was launched in 1988. And so I kept in touch with Honda and towards the end of the year they said I could have a production RC30. They also said that if someone could come up with about £6000, they would give me another RC30 complete with a Formula One kit to upgrade it for the quality racing classes.

Jim Oliver agreed to pay for the F1 kit and Honda also offered me a CBR600 so that I could ride in the CBR Challenge on the mainland as well as in the 600cc Production and Formula Two races at the TT. It all sounded great but being promised bikes is one thing and actually taking delivery of them is another as I was about to find out.

Anyway, the rest of the 1987 season went okay for me and I picked up some more wins at Oliver's Mount, Knockhill, Cadwell Park and Jurby, which is a short airfield circuit on the Isle of Man.

Short-circuit racing requires a totally different style of riding compared to the TT. For starters, you're riding elbow to elbow with 20 other guys pushing and jostling for position whereas at the TT you're on your own. You can also afford to fall off more often because there's generally lots of run-off space enabling you to take greater risks, whereas if you take a risk on the Island you're into a brick wall more often than not. On top of that, there's the fact that short-circuit surfaces are a lot smoother and offer more grip so you can corner faster and lean the bike over to a greater degree.

Because of these and other differences, very few riders have been good at both disciplines, especially in more recent years since the TT has lost its prestige and there's less incentive to have a go at pure road racing. Carl Fogarty is one exception and Michael Rutter is another: they have both proved to be good road racers and good short-circuit riders and I'm the same in that I never had a problem changing my style to suit either discipline

In fact, I thought the two disciplines could complement each other. Towards the end of 1985, I realized I would have to do some further short-circuit racing if my TT results were to improve. I felt I needed to ride more aggressively and to attack the course more and I could only learn that sort of style by scratching round purpose-built racetracks neck and neck with other riders. My theory worked as my results really picked up at the TT after I started full-time short circuit racing in 1986.

Many riders say they don't ride the TT course as hard as they ride short circuits but that's absolute bollocks. If we didn't, why would there be crashes? Why would we be suffering huge tank-slappers at various points around the course? Why would there be huge dark lines of rubber exiting corners as riders wind on the gas to the max and get the rear wheel spinning up? There are lots of TT videos showing riders such as Carl Fogarty, Phillip McCallen and myself getting bikes all crossed up because we're trying so hard. Have a look at any one of those videos and you'll see what I mean. There's a lot of money at stake at the TT (well, there is nowadays anyway) and there's only one TT each year so there's also a lot at stake as far as sponsors and manufacturers are concerned. You simply can't afford to ride well within your limits or you're going to be left behind.

Admittedly, the style of riding is different in that you can't use every inch of the road as you do on a short circuit but even that's not always the case. Watch riders exiting the Gooseneck and you'll see them skimming the grass banking. And I used to use the bus stop at Schoolhouse Corner to give me a few more inches of tarmac when I needed it. The sheer bumpiness of the course means you can't take some corners as hard as you would if they were smooth like a short circuit but generally speaking, if someone says they're riding at 80 per cent of their abilities and still winning TTs, they're lying. If you want to win a race on the Isle of Man you'd better be prepared to ride flat out, make no mistake.

Over the next few years, I would ride the course faster than any man in history.

The Impossible Dream

'I laughed when they asked me to ride a Norton at the TT.'

To understand fully all the implications of my 1992 Senior TT victory, which remains one of my greatest ever triumphs, I'll need to mention the 1991 TT.

I was still living on the Isle of Man with my girlfriend, Lesley Henthorn, at the time and her neighbour was away on holiday so we arranged for Foggy and Michaela to stay at her house. Michaela was pregnant with Danielle at the time and I remember us all sitting around sunbathing and having a great time – while the press were saying we hated each other and refused to speak to one another!

But there was a lot of pressure on Carl and I that year because Honda had shipped in some really exotic, one-off bikes for us to make sure they won the Formula One TT as that would give them 10 F1 wins in a row. They didn't care which one of us won it but one of us *had* to.

We were busting each other's guts during practice

week as I would put in a 121mph lap then Carl would go out and do a 122mph lap. Then I'd go out and lap at 123mph and it went on like that all week. These were speeds that no one had ever seen round the TT course before and we were breaking records almost every time we went out for a lap.

Mr Oguma, the chief of HRC (Honda Racing Corporation) had come over to the Island from Japan and he was going mental at our antics, terrified that we were going to crash and kill ourselves. He called a meeting and sat Foggy and I down at a table like naughty little school children. We got a real bollocking for going so fast; apparently we'd scared Oguma-san shitless when he watched us at the bottom of Bray Hill! He was a fierce-looking man and he pointed a big, stubby finger at both of us in turn and shouted, 'You and you, not enemies. Honda and Yamaha are enemies. Honda and Suzuki are enemies. Honda and Kawasaki are enemies. You two not enemies. Must decide now which one will win big race.'

So there we were, both completely determined to win the Formula One race and we were being told to draw lots over it. No way! As we left that office I said to Carl, 'I had a shit TT last year and there's no way I'm going to lose this.' Carl was equally determined to win so we agreed between us that the first man to reach the finish line would be the victor; there was just no way either of us were going to concede that race without a fight.

The morning of that 1991 Formula One TT was the most tense experience I've ever had in racing.

Michaela Fogarty came over to me on the start line and said, 'Steve, you're a bit more sensible than that idiot (meaning Carl). You'll back off if it gets scary won't you?' I was thinking, 'No bloody way will I,' but I just nodded sweetly to reassure her.

There was so much adrenaline pumping as Foggy and I both knew we'd have to ride round the most dangerous circuit in the world faster than anyone else had ever done before if we wanted to win. And boy did we both want to win.

As it turned out I had the race won in the first 10 miles because my tactics were to go flat out from the start to try and get a gap on Carl and mentally defeat him. At the thirteenth Milestone, my board came out and said '+5 seconds' and I could just visualize Foggy seeing a minus five signal and imagined how demoralizing that would be for him. I caught him on the road on lap two at Ballaugh Bridge as I'd made up the 30-second starting-time difference and for a while we raced neck and neck on the roads. Carl had some kind of problem with his bike cutting out at high speeds but I didn't care; I won by over 40 seconds and set a new outright lap record at 123.48mph. It was a brilliant race as we were wheel to wheel on the road all through laps three and four which was great fun and good for the spectators.

Foggy didn't ride in the Senior race the following Friday because he was off on World Superbike duty so Joey Dunlop got his RVF. I beat Joey by 80 seconds after catching him on the road towards the end of the last lap. It was really nice to ride alongside him and put on a show for the crowds but to be honest, I wish Carl had been there to push me.

I won the Supersport 600 race that week too so it was a brilliant TT for me apart from my usual Junior jinx; this time the bike seized solid at the start of the second lap. But the important points to take away from that meeting were that I'd beaten Carl on an identical bike and I knew he wasn't happy about it. I knew we would never again have such exotic machinery at our disposal for the TT. We were unlikely ever to be on identical bikes again either so it looked like being the last time Carl and I would have a head-to-head on the Island, especially as Foggy and I both said we'd never be back to race there again.

Well, we did come back for different reasons and the 1992 Senior race is still talked about today as one of the best ever seen in the long history of the Tourist Trophy. It was the fastest race in the history of the event as well as being one of the closest and Foggy set a new lap record during it which wasn't bettered for seven years. But most of all it's remembered because a small British team on a shoestring budget won the race with a British bike which started life as a crazy project in the back of a shed.

It's hard to believe now that I actually laughed when Norton's team boss, Barry Symmons, asked me to ride that bike at the TT but I did. I thought, 'You must be joking – that thing will never last one lap of the Isle of Man.'

By winning that race on the Norton by just four seconds from Foggy, I beat not only Carl but also the might of Honda, Yamaha and all the other teams. I also created history by becoming the first rider to win the Senior TT on a British bike since the late, great Mike Hailwood in 1961.

For the team and myself the victory was a dream come true. We'd had just one month to raise the £25,000 needed to compete. Furthermore, I had only completed eight laps of testing before arriving at the TT (We couldn't do any more because the bike blew up!) and no one had thought we had a chance of even finishing the race, never mind winning it. And the 40,000 patriotic spectators who had made the journey over to the Isle of Man went absolutely wild at the sight of a British bike back on top of the world again – it was a real throwback to the 1960s when the British bike industry led the world. There was hardly a dry eye on the whole island.

That night I went into Douglas and got absolutely legless. I was even caught by the TV cameras singing the worst karaoke rendition of *Country Roads* ever heard, but I didn't care. As far as I was concerned, I had achieved the impossible and deserved to get drunk. So I did.

I made the most of my night out and all the media attention the win had attracted because it had been a bloody long, hard slog to achieve it. At one point I didn't think I'd be riding at the TT at all because in the space of just six months, I had been dropped by Honda, joined Yamaha, and then left them one month before the race because I didn't feel they were giving me enough support.

When Foggy decided to leave Honda to go World Superbike racing on a private Ducati in 1992, Honda thought I was the right man to replace him. Team boss Neil Tuxworth sat me down at the end of '91 and said I should give up my 250cc racing and ride Honda's 750cc RC30 in the British championships and at the TT. He offered me two bikes, a full squad with good mechanics, the whole deal. I thought it sounded fantastic but the more I pushed for a contract over winter, the less I heard from Tuxworth. Honda had me on a promise and so I didn't look anywhere else for a ride. But when I finally managed to speak to him in early January of 1992 he was very abrupt and just told me that there was a letter in the post then put the phone down on me.

In hindsight he was probably embarrassed by their U-turn and decision to sign Simon Crafar after an impressive Honda ride at Brands Hatch, but when I received the letter the following day I couldn't believe what I was reading. In a nutshell, it stated that Honda no longer required my services. What? I'd won seven TTs for Honda as well as the British 250cc championship, then they'd promised me the earth for 1992 just to turn round and slap me in the face like that. I thought, 'Bugger me, they've dropped me right in it.' Honda had opted to employ Kiwi rider Simon Crafar instead of me because he'd put in one good performance at Brands Hatch towards the end of 1991. Loyalty works only one way in bike racing.

Anyway, I thought, 'What the hell am I going to do now?' All the other good rides had been taken and it looked like I was going to be left out in the cold for most of the '92 season. The only thing I managed to arrange was a ride with Kawasaki France in the world endurance championship but that was for just five races over the whole season and, although I enjoyed endurance racing it wasn't really the way I wanted my career to go.

Eventually I got a call from Andy Smith at Yamaha saying he would love to give me a bike for the TT. That was fair enough but I told him that I needed a bike for the whole season, not just for one event. Andy eventually agreed to supply me with two good 750cc bikes and a good mechanic for the British championships, to be run under a dealer-supported team called Tillston's Yamaha, as well as a 600cc production bike and 250cc race bike for the TT. Things were looking good again.

But when I actually tried to get hold of the special parts I'd been promised, things started falling apart. Rob McElnea, a former Grand Prix racer and TT winner who was running the official Loctite Yamaha team as well as riding in it, refused to give Tillston's the parts saying he needed them for his own team. I called Yamaha straight away and asked what was going on. Andy Smith told me to leave things with him but weeks went by before we got any equipment and it was obvious straight away that it wasn't what we'd been promised. The bikes and parts were outdated and that's when alarm bells really started ringing.

I raced at Oulton Park early in the season and could only manage seventh because the Yamahas I had were so uncompetitive, but at least I beat Crafar on the Honda that should have been mine. Still, I wasn't happy and had no interest in riding under-par bikes all season. Yamaha had paid me a £10,000 retainer to race for them at the TT but I was prepared to give it back and not ride for them if they wouldn't give me better parts for my British championship bike.

That was a big sacrifice for me as I wasn't being paid to race in the British championship that year – the only money I got was a couple of grand for wearing an Arai helmet. I was hoping to earn some good prize money at the TT to supplement my meagre income so it was really important for me to race there even though I'd said I would never go back.

When I gave Andy Smith my ultimatum – give me some parts or I'm backing out of the TT – he said, 'You won't do that Steve,' but I thought, 'Just you bloody watch me.' I was really pissed off so I phoned my friend Michael Brandon from Abus Locks, a bike security firm based in Hawick. Michael was one of the sponsors of the Kawasaki team, which was fielding John Reynolds and Brian Morrison that year and when I told him I was thinking of throwing the towel in with Yamaha and didn't know what I was going to ride he said, 'Leave it with me. I'll see what I can do.'

The next morning he called and said he'd arranged a Kawasaki for me to ride at the weekend. Reynolds was cleaning up in the British championships on the Kawasaki so I knew it was a good bike and because I was contracted with Kawasaki France for the world endurance races I even had some Kawasaki leathers!

I was told to turn up at Donington Park with my leathers and that John Reynolds's spare bike would be waiting for me. It sounded perfect so I called Andy Smith at Yamaha as promised and when he said there was still no word on any better equipment, I told him I'd be posting his £10,000 cheque back to him and he could stick it where he wanted. I'd had enough of being fobbed off.

As a supposed Yamaha rider I turned a few heads in the paddock at Donington Park in my Kawasaki leathers but none more so than Barry Symmons's who was managing the JPS Norton team with Ron Haslam and Robert Dunlop as his riders. I told him the story about Yamaha and the TT and I could almost see his brain going into overdrive straight away. He had been looking for someone to ride Haslam's Norton at the TT. Haslam had a broken leg at the time but he wouldn't have been going to the Isle of Man anyway so Barry was sniffing around for another rider. He told me, 'Christ, let's get you on the Norton for the TT. That would be awesome.'

I provisionally agreed to it since I had no other offers but inside I was thinking it was a bit of a joke. I'd always seen the Norton as a kind of wacky project bike and didn't think there was any chance it would last six laps of the punishing TT course. After all, a guy called Brian Crichton had developed it from a slow, old, Norton police bike in the back of a shed. Surely it couldn't win a TT race?

I finished sixth at Donington on the Kawasaki and

then was second at Brands Hatch the following day
as I got more used to the bike. After that race two
mechanics that I knew, called Dave Collins and Jeff
Tollan, approached me and asked if I'd be interested
in riding in the Malaysian Superbike championship.
They were running a Kawasaki team there with Kiwi
rider Andrew Stroud and asked if I'd fly out to test
their bike. With nothing else on offer I agreed and flew
out to the Shah Alam Grand Prix circuit for some
tests. What I'd forgotten was that the circuit was
notorious for snakes and I hate snakes – I mean I'm
fucking terrified of them – but I just tried to put them
out of my mind and get on with the job in hand.

We unloaded the bike from the van amid all these
little Indian and Malaysian boys running around
the paddock and that's when I realized it was a track
day open to the public rather than a private test day
which is more usual when testing a race bike. Now,
here in the UK, track days are populated by riders
with full-on sports bikes capable of 160mph but in
Malaysia, the only bikes were little souped-up, step-
through scooters such as Honda C90s and the like.
They called them 'Underbones' for some reason and
there were hundreds of them, all with a top speed of
about 80mph so it was going to be difficult to navi-
gate between them all but at least I could be sure of
being fastest.

Anyway, the track finally went quiet for a while so
I headed out and took it easy as I felt my way round
for the first time and I was just hooking into fourth
gear round the back of the circuit when this bloody

great cobra slithered across the tarmac! I was terrified and gassed the bike as if my life depended on it to get the hell out of there – I probably went through that corner quicker than any rider before or since to get away from that snake.

I pulled straight into the pits and shouted at the guys, 'There's a snake on the track, there's a fucking snake on the track! I'm not going back out there,' but they all just laughed and sent me out again saying it would be gone by the time I got back round. I didn't see the slithery bastard again so I started laying down some good lap times and was really sliding the bike around because the high temperatures were just destroying the tyres, but I loved every minute of it.

In my first Malaysian races I got a first and second place which I was pretty pleased with because there were some very good Australian riders there like Chris Haldane on a Marlboro Yamaha and Trevor Jordan who rode for Lucky Strike Kawasaki. After that I was offered a ride for the rest of the championship at a rate of £3000 a round on top of all expenses. The prize money was crap, just a few bloody roubles or something daft like that, but it was worth it for the laughs we had and I eventually ended the season in third spot, which I was quite happy with.

Barry Symmons worked feverishly trying to sort out the Norton TT deal while I was testing in Malaysia. The biggest problem was that we needed to raise £25,000 to cover costs and there was less than one month from the time that we first discussed the idea to the start of practice. The people from cigarette firm JPS, who normally sponsored the bike in the British championships, weren't interested for some reason so I called my old friend Michael Brandon again and explained the situation.

I was desperate to ride the bike by now, not because I thought it could win, but because I really thought it could be the making of me as far as publicity went. Public interest in the British Norton was huge and I knew there would be even more nostalgia about it at the TT where they used to go so well decades ago; in fact, Rem Fowler won a TT on a Norton in the event's very first year in 1907. I just felt it would really put me back in the spotlight and that was something I needed badly if only to secure a solid ride for 1993.

Anyway, Michael Brandon got his head together with Andy Freeman at EBC brakes and together they reckoned they could raise about £10,000. That was brilliant but we still needed another £15,000. A deal was being arranged with Manx Telecom for the extra money but they pulled the plug at the eleventh hour and we were left in the lurch again.

Then, at the very last minute, I approached Brian Kreisky who produced TV coverage for the TT races and told him I would put cameras on the bike or do whatever he wanted filming-wise if he would help with our effort. Brian had good relations with the Isle of Man Tourist Board so he took me to see them and we sat down to try and get some money. Brian was amazing in the way he twisted their arms up their backs and persuaded the board to sponsor us.

They eventually came up with around £10,000 which was still a bit short but Barry Symmons did some calculations and said, 'That's enough, that'll do, we'll be there boys. We're going racing.' It was a real *Rocky* moment.

So I finally got to test the Norton for the first (and only) time at Oulton Park on the Thursday before TT practice started when most racers were already on their way to the Isle of Man. The team told me there were a few things they wanted to try on the bike so I said fair enough and out I went, eager to see what the Norton was like. As I got to the first proper corner I went to gently tip the bike in and the bloody thing nearly fell on its side. I thought, 'Fuckin' hell, what's this all about?' I'd never ridden a bike that steered so quickly. Much too quickly in fact. It nearly pissed off and took the corner by itself.

Apparently, that's the way Ron Haslam liked his bikes set up for short circuits but there's no way you can ride the TT with a bike set up as nervously as that. Stability is everything on the Island and I knew we had to make some vital changes but the team's suspension guru, Ron Williams, argued that the bike didn't need changing and he actually got quite stroppy about the whole thing.

Eventually, Ron allowed the mechanics to lessen the severity of the steering and it felt a little bit better but then after six more laps, just as I was getting used to the thing, the engine locked up solid. The team had been trying some kind of turbo system on it and it was just too much so the engine cried enough and that was it. That was all the practice I had on the Norton before the TT.

In total I'd done about eight laps and when I came back into the pits everyone asked me what I thought of the bike. I said, 'Boys, to be quite honest I don't think that thing will ever last one lap of the TT, never mind six. It can't even manage 10 laps round Oulton Park without shitting its pants.'

Anyway, I flew over to the Isle of Man and when the team arrived Barry said I could make some more changes to the steering. Apparently he'd had a word with Ron Williams and explained that it was my neck on the line and therefore I should be allowed to set the bike up the way I wanted to.

The first practice session got underway at 6pm on Monday evening in miserable wet conditions and to everyone's surprise, I ended up at the top of the practice leaderboard ahead of Foggy, who was riding the Yamaha OWO1 which I had originally been meant to ride.

He was desperate for cash to fund his privateer World Superbike campaign so he'd accepted the ride on that basis, even though he didn't really want to ride at the TT again.

The rest of practice week was a wash out weatherwise but when I woke up on the Saturday morning for the Formula One race, the sun was beating down and conditions were perfect. Well, they were perfect for sunbathers and ice cream salesmen but not for my Norton. On the very first lap it started overheating in the hot conditions and I had to keep a close eye on the temperature gauge from then on. Robert Dunlop's JPS Norton expired completely on the first lap, which wasn't exactly encouraging.

I came in after the second lap for my pit stop and my crew ripped the front mudguard off to allow more air into the radiator but that cost me about 20 seconds and Foggy was long gone by then. His glory was short lived though because he was so hard on his Yamaha that he broke the gearbox on the fifth lap and handed the win to Phillip McCallen on the factory Honda.

By the time I got out of the pits and got going again, the bike was weaving all over the road and I had to fight it all the way round, constantly trying to analyse the instability problem. But the top speed was awesome and I really started enjoying myself and clawed back as much time on McCallen as I could in the remaining laps to finish second.

After that I was pretty convinced that if we could sort out the problems with the bike during the week, I stood a real chance of winning the big one – the Senior TT held on the Friday. We took the bike up to Jurby, a disused runway on the Isle of Man, and got to work. One problem I had in the race was that the wind was pushing my body back on the bike and this meant I was pulling the front forks up and making the rear suspension squat at the same time. That meant there was no weight over the front of the bike, which in turn made it unstable. We got round the problem by simply fitting a taller screen so I could get really tucked in out of the air.

We certainly never lacked top speed; the Norton

was tremendously fast in a straight line and a radar gun clocked me at 193mph down Sulby straight at one point. But it was the weirdest bike to ride because of its rotary engine. It had very little engine braking and I just got sucked really deep into corners so I had to change all the braking points that I used on 'normal' bikes. I remember many times I was hammering down the gearbox and pulling the front brake lever like hell only to find I was still heading into the corners way too fast.

Anyway, between the Formula One and Senior races we added the taller screen, ditched the front mudguard, added wider and higher bars to help stability over the bumps and made some little fork protectors to stop them getting chipped with stones now that the mudguard was gone. With those changes made, the bike was stripped and every single component checked and rechecked to enhance our chances of making it to the finish line. Then all we could do was wait until Friday.

A Day at the Races

'For the first time in my life I thought victory maybe wasn't as important as living.'

Under a baking hot sun and a cloudless blue sky I lined up on the famous Glencrutchery Road start line for the 1992 Senior TT.

Carl Fogarty was starting at number four and I would set off at number 19, three minutes behind him.

I'd finished second three times that week and was desperate for a win at this point, especially on the Norton as I was fully aware of how important that would be for my career.

Earlier I'd been chatting to a spectator who said I looked like I was trying too hard in the F1 race and he thought that was what was actually slowing me down. Smoothness and consistency are the key factors round the Isle of Man so I decided to ease myself into the race rather than go gung-ho from the start.

The first signal I got was 13 miles out and it told me I was in second place. I had expected to be fourth or fifth at the pace I was riding but there I was only two seconds off the leader and I knew it had to be Carl. Even though there were other top names like Joey Dunlop, Phillip McCallen, Robert Dunlop and Trevor Nation in the race, I'd no doubt it was Foggy who was leading. No one else could touch us at that pace so I didn't give the others a second thought.

Foggy was still leading after the first 37.74 miles lap and he'd posted an average speed of 121.90mph from a standing start. We were setting an amazing pace on bikes that were really quite inferior to the factory Hondas of the previous year.

I started to up my pace on the second lap having found a rhythm and I set about trying to catch Carl. By the end of the lap I was 2.8 seconds ahead as we pulled in for our first pit stops. I took the precaution of fitting a new rear tyre because I didn't know how badly those speeds would tear up the rubber. Foggy only took on fuel and blasted out of pit lane having retaken the lead with his quicker stop. Once again, I had to do all the work of catching him up and I knew I'd have to ride really hard from then on.

I got back on the gas but was still treating the bike with respect. In the F1 race I'd tried to ride it flat out everywhere but it was simply too fast on top speed for that and I had been totally out of control. This time I was in control of the bike instead of having it take me for a ride. But I was still hitting bumps and getting lifted up out of my seat and the wind at those speeds was really wrenching at my neck and shoulders, threatening to blow me off the back of the bike. Bigger bumps caused the bike to shake its head viciously from side to side while gentle rises in the road sent the front wheel skyward, which is always dangerous because the wind can get under the front wheel and loop the bike over.

By the end of the third lap I'd pulled back five seconds on Foggy and was just one second behind him. I knew that would demoralize him and play on his mind but I kept charging all the same.

Because of my low starting number I had to pass lots of slower riders and they can be a real threat round the TT course as they've no idea when someone's behind them. They can move right over in front of you in a corner at the last moment and force you to squeeze between them and a stone wall to get by. Sometimes I revved my throttle like mad to let them know I was there but it's not always possible if you're already flat out and have no more revs left.

At the end of the fourth lap as we came in for our pit stops I was 7.4 seconds in the lead. I wiped my visor clean of flies while the team refueled the bike. Races can be won or lost in the pits and it's a precise art, which my team and I had practised in the garage time after time to get right. We worked on ways to save fractions of seconds here and there. Our solution was simple – keep it to the basics. The more things we changed, the more could go wrong. Some riders change visors and earplugs and some even change helmets but I didn't do any of that. I cleaned my own visor, which meant there was one less person to get in the way, took a quick drink through a bottle with a long straw attached to rehydrate and let my mechanics get on with dumping the fuel in.

But no amount of practice can account for nerves. My team was so tense and so desperate to win the race that one of the mechanics fumbled with the petrol cap and we lost vital seconds. It took team boss Barry Symmons to interject and tell everyone to slow down before the cap was popped into place and I was push-started down pit lane again.

The stop took me 35 seconds which was way too long and it left me just one second ahead of Fogarty after all the hard work I'd put in to catch and pass him on corrected time.

Seven miles out at Ballacraine, Foggy had pulled out a lead of three seconds over me but by Ramsey on the fifth lap I had overtaken him again and pulled out a lead of 6.4 seconds. I knew Carl would struggle to pull that back in one lap but I also knew how good he was and that it was still a possibility. I only had to make one slight error and he'd be right back on me. There was no doubt in my mind that he'd try everything that he knew on that final circuit.

Carl and I had already shattered the lap record I set the year before on the Honda RVF, which was a measure of how hard we were trying. But Foggy pulled out all the stops on the last circuit to set a new outright lap record at an amazing 123.61mph. It was such a fast time that it stood for seven years.

The crowd was awesome throughout the race but I'd never seen anything like it on my final circuit. It must have been incredible for all those fans to see a

British bike threatening to win the Senior TT after more than 30 years and it was very hard not to be distracted by them. Every vantage point was packed with fans hanging out onto the road, waving their programmes, cheering and taking photographs – it was a spectacular sight.

On the last few miles I started talking to the bike, urging it home, nursing it every inch and mile of the way. I was well aware that I'd been unlucky in many races at the TT before and it was quite possible that the Norton could just blow up any minute at the pace I was riding. More than 226 miles flat out over bumpy roads with six climbs over the 2197 feet Snaefell mountain is a lot to ask of any bike, let alone a low budget, privately funded one.

As Foggy crossed the finish line he had a three-minute wait for me to come home to find out who had won. He'd given it everything but now all he could do was wait. As I reached Signpost corner just a few miles from home the traditional light came on at the start/finish grandstand to indicate that I was nearly there. The crowd was going absolutely mental sensing that the Norton was surely going to hold out. As I crossed the finish line and slammed on the anchors I still didn't know who had won but as soon as I saw the crowds lining the path that leads back to the pits I knew I'd done it. I remember my back being sore from all the slaps I got even though I had a back protector on. I was totally swamped the second I got off the bike and I had to push through the crowds to give Lesley a hug and a kiss. Then the throng of enthusiasts inadvertently pushed her against the bike's still red-hot exhaust and she needed first aid treatment for the burn.

Bike racing doesn't usually attract an awful lot of mainstream press but that was a fairy-tale win and there were reporters present from all the national newspapers who would never normally cover a bike race. The British bike angle itself created a lot of interest but the shoestring budget nature of the team made it even better. The fact that I'd achieved something that had not been done for over 30 years and at speeds that had never been seen before just made it all the better.

It was the fastest race in TT history with my average speed for the entire six laps being 121.28mph. Foggy may have set a new outright lap record on the last lap but it still wasn't enough to beat me – I don't think anyone in the world could have beaten me that day.

My team was ecstatic. They knew the budget was running out and that this might be the last big win for them; it was certainly the biggest they'd ever achieved. When the press asked Barry Symmons if we'd be having a party to celebrate he replied, 'If we can afford it.' That's how tight things were money-wise. But none of that mattered; we'd silenced a thousand critics and made racing history in what was probably the greatest single race of my life.

I must admit there was a tear in my eye as I fully realized what I'd achieved and people are still talking about that race to this day. Most rank it alongside

Giacomo Agostini and Mike Hailwood's epic duel in 1967 as the best race ever held on the Island and that's about as high a praise as you can get.

After the dust had settled Foggy once again announced he would never return to the TT as it was now just too fast and dangerous and this time he kept his word. I agreed and said I wouldn't be back either. There seemed little point if Foggy wasn't going to be there – he was the only guy who really provided me with a challenge.

By the end of the year the JPS Norton team had ran out of steam and cash and the bikes were put into storage. It was all over. So many things came together at the right time to make the 1992 TT something really special and many of them were never seen there again.

I was dying to hear Carl's side of the story so we got together after the race to swap tales and it was uncanny how similar his experiences had been to mine. The one section of the track that had been scaring me badly was a straight between Kerrowmoar and Glentramman, which is probably the bumpiest part of the TT course. It should be taken flat out, pinned in sixth gear at about 180mph but I was having to back off a bit because my bike was tying itself in knots and threatening to chuck me over a hedge. I was really pissed off because on every lap through that section I was thinking, 'Fuckin' hell, Foggy will be getting away from me, come on, come on Steve.' But there was nothing I could do about it because the bike just couldn't cope with the vicious bumps at those speeds. I was riding it beyond its limits and it was going into such a weave that I was totally out of control at 180mph, just hanging on and praying for the best. At that speed, instinct takes over and for the first time in my life, I actually started thinking that maybe victory wasn't as important as living but that soon passed and I got my head down again.

However, before I even mentioned this to Carl he told me that he had been really mad because on every lap he was forced to shut the throttle off a bit on one particular section of the course, and he thought I would be gaining a few tenths of a second on him each time. I couldn't believe it when he told me that, as it was exactly the same section of the course where I was having the identical problem!

That's how closely matched we were and how close we were to the limit – we simply couldn't have gone any faster with the technology of the bikes at the time. Carl had been so determined to beat me in that race because we'd been on equal bikes the year before and I'd won, so he was out for revenge. I wanted to beat him fair and square too, especially as everyone had been bitching about me and Carl having the best bikes in 1991. They said we were only winning because of our bikes so I suppose it was a good thing that we both had average bikes for 1992 just to prove a point.

Foggy's Yamaha was nothing special and I've already explained about my Norton but we still kicked everyone else's arses and proved our speed was nothing to do with the machines we were on. Even so,

I couldn't believe that I'd won on the very project bike that I used to laugh at!

Although everyone in the sport congratulated me on my Norton win and the press loved the 'David and Goliath' sentiment of it all, I wasn't exactly inundated with calls offering me rides on the short circuits as I'd hoped to be. Still, 1992 had turned out okay for me even though I had been living from hand to mouth and taking any rides I could just to keep my hand in.

Initially, it looked like it was going to be a great season with Honda until they fucked me up big style by dropping me from their plans and after that it was just a case of picking up the scraps. That's why I couldn't believe it when, at the end of the year, Neil called me up out of the blue again and asked me what I was doing in 1993. I said, 'Nowt. Why do you want to know anyway?' Then he told me that Honda Japan was sending one of their exotic factory RVFs across to Honda Britain and he asked me if I wanted to ride it. I thought, 'You've got to be taking the piss.' I was back to where I'd started.

Sacked

'He loaded the gun and got Roger to pull the trigger.'

I don't remember breaking a mirror in 1996 but I certainly started a run of bad luck as far as the British championship was concerned.

After winning the title in 1995 I didn't complete another full season uninterrupted until 2002 due either to teams folding or sacking me plus a whole catalogue of physical injuries. If you plotted a chart of the highs and lows of those seven years for me it would look like a map of the Himalayas.

It all started when Steve Horton, the promoter of the Devimead Ducati team, told me he had arranged factory Kawasakis for the 1996 season and was going to set up a new outfit called Nemesis Kawasaki. He had new workshops, a top mechanic in Stewart Johnstone, a good truck – the whole deal.

I still wanted to go racing but I was so loved up with Kelly that I was living in my own little world on the Isle of Man and I probably didn't take enough interest in what was going on with the team. Whenever Steve called with more details I just agreed and got back to my love life as soon as I could. That turned out to be a big mistake.

The season actually started OK for me with a second place at Donington Park but from then on it was downhill. As the other teams developed their bikes and the race pace picked up, we got left behind because we didn't have the money to improve our bikes. Kawasaki had given us the machines and the race kits but it was the team's responsibility to fund any developmental work and the funds just weren't there to accommodate that. Unfortunately that outfit was built on dreams and an empty purse.

As a measure of how poorly organized the team was (it was eventually dubbed 'In-a-mess' Kawasaki by the biking press), Stewart Johnstone left before the season started and I even arrived at Mallory for a test day on one occasion to find that no one else had bothered turning up because the bikes weren't ready!

My bike blew up spectacularly in the second race at Donington right in front of the TV cameras, then I had problems with grip at Thruxton and salvaged only a couple of sixth places. A crash and a fifth at Oulton Park didn't help matters, then I finished tenth and ninth at Snetterton before the inevitable happened and the team finally folded at the Brands Hatch round. It was the second team that had collapsed around me in a matter of months.

Luckily for me however, Reve Kawasaki team

owner, Ben Atkins, still had his bikes and the entire infrastructure to restart his team even though he hadn't fielded anyone in the 1996 British championship up to that point. He had made arrangements for Jim Moodie to have a ride at the TT then decided to offer me a ride when he heard my team had collapsed. I took Red Bull (who had been backing me in the Nemesis team) to Ben's team as sponsors and they ended up staying with him right up until 2001.

At the end of July I accepted his offer and we were up and running in time for the Knockhill round, which was awesome. As soon as I got there I put in 40 laps to get used to the bike and ended up being the fastest in that first session. I was quickest the next day, too, ahead of Niall Mackenzie and Jamie Whitham (who had made a full recovery from cancer) on the Cadbury's Boost Yamahas and they had been dominating the whole season, so it was great to get one over on them.

I finished third in both races which, considering I'd not raced the bike before, was great and a big difference from the tenth places I had been posting on the Nemesis bike. When we got to Cadwell Park I was fastest again and set pole position for the race proving that my riding wasn't at fault. I had just been hindered by poor machinery.

I finished the first race in third place behind Whitham and Mackenzie and was fifth in the second leg but still really chuffed with my efforts, and I actually beat Mackenzie to second place at Mallory then took another third in the second race there. I'm sure if I'd had the Reve Kawasaki for the whole season I could have challenged for the championship but that's by-the-by.

As it was, I ended the season in fifth place overall after getting on the podium at Donington Park again in the final round. That's the difference a decent team can make; Ben's squad was organized, the bikes were well prepared and all I had to do was ride, which is how it should be. I got on well with Ben, too, and that's how I ended up riding for him again the following season. At that point he was happy with me but that was all to change before too long.

I was annoyed with the way 1996 went because I felt I'd wasted a lot of time with the Nemesis squad when I should have been challenging for race wins. So when Ben said he would be running Ducatis under Red Bull sponsorship in 1997 I was definitely up for it and felt sure I could make amends for what had been a miserable title defence.

During the winter, I moved out of my modest semi-detached bachelor pad and a bought a much bigger place for Kelly and I. It was a beautiful house and I still regret the fact that I had to move out when I split up with her in 2001 but I'll get to that later.

I was massively pumped up for the 1997 season as I felt I had the best team ever with four ex-factory Ducatis, huge team trucks, big sponsorship and great team personnel. My team-mate was to be John Reynolds who was coming back to the UK after struggling on a Suzuki in World Superbikes. John and Ben Atkins were the best of mates and that began to tell later in the season but at the start of the year it looked like being a dream team.

But my hopes were soon to be shattered as I struggled to adapt to the Ducati. It felt like a completely different machine to the one that I'd won the 1995 title on, as it was a lot more aggressive in the way it made its power. The bike had been designed around WSB rider John Kocinski's recommendations and the chassis was just crap. Foggy had the same sort of complaints when he went back to Ducati after riding for Honda in 1996 – the 1995 model had been far superior.

Our first test session was at Mallory Park and after building up the laps running the bike in I was just starting to gas it a bit. To my horror, as I rode through the Esses the throttle stuck open and I had no choice but to brake as hard as I could to lock the front wheel, lay the bike down and pray as I headed straight for the Armco wall. I was knocked unconscious and spent the night in Leicester Royal Infirmary.

I didn't do much physical damage apart from cracking my shoulder but that crash had a bit of a lasting psychological effect through the season as I lost a lot of faith in the bike. We went testing again but the Ducati still felt too aggressive and I couldn't get the power down smoothly which is the key to my riding style. It was really 'loose' too and by that I mean it was sliding and bucking and weaving everywhere which is not only unsettling for the rider but it wastes time too.

John was turning in better times than I was but he was riding by the seat of his pants and looked like an accident waiting to happen. I don't think a rider should have to do that to get results; if a bike can't be set up to run properly it shouldn't be on a bloody racetrack in the first place.

I told the team we needed to smooth out the power delivery and get some suspension experts to work on the damping. Ben refused to make those changes. It seems that he did not think the bikes were dangerous, thought I was making a fuss and pointed to John as an example that the bike was fine. He would say, 'John's getting results, why can't you?' But John was either getting a result or crashing and I didn't want to do that. It's dangerous for the rider and expensive for the team too so I couldn't understand why Ben just wouldn't make those changes. That way I could have gone faster and I wouldn't have racked up a big repair bill either.

Again, just like the year before, my season started OK with a third place at Donington Park and a fourth at Oulton Park, both circuits on which I always tend to go well at. But from there on it was downhill again and I started finishing well down the points with a thirteenth at Snetterton and an eleventh place at Brands Hatch. I was sick of banging my head on a brick wall because no one would allow me to make the changes to the bike which I knew would make it much more rideable. Eventually I just lost heart in the whole deal and gave up trying.

Matters came to a head at Thruxton where I finished twelfth in the first leg and pulled out of the second race with one lap to go. Everyone thinks I finished last in that race but in truth I didn't even finish it – the organizers and all the results sheets showed me as finishing eighteenth, and last, because they credited me with finishing the race even though I pulled in with one lap still to go.

After that race my team manager Roger Marshall, against whom I used to race at the TT, came into my motorhome and I knew by the look on his face that something was very wrong. I expected some dissatisfaction over my poor results but Roger looked very solemn. He sat down and said something like, 'Steve, we can't afford to have another embarrassing result like that' so I thought, 'Great, they're going to let me change the bikes.' Wrong! He proceeded to tell me that the team was going to have to replace me because of my bad results. I suppose I should have been expecting it but it still came as a bit of a shock. I felt a bit sorry for Roger because he'd been given the dirty work to do. As Ben had hired me I would have expected him to deliver the news but he didn't even have the bollocks to come and tell me himself, he simply loaded the gun and got Roger to pull the trigger.

A racing paddock is a very small place so it's impossible to avoid seeing people that you're pissed off with. I've learned that it's easier just to smile and pretend nothing's happened and that's pretty much what I did the next time I saw Ben Atkins. There's no point taking the huff or shouting and screaming at anyone because you can't avoid them after that.

The only way you can really hit back at someone who's sacked you is to get another ride and go like hell, hoping you can beat the riders from your old team. I always ride out of my skin on occasions like that and it's always worked for me. It's a great feeling being able to prove that it was the bike and not me that was the problem.

So although being sacked came as a bit of a shock, I realized there was no point in continuing with a team that wouldn't allow me to make vital changes to the bike and seemed to think I should risk my life to get a result.

The other problem in that team was favouritism. I like John Reynolds and have nothing against him but he was like a son to Ben Atkins and he was his blue-eyed boy who got all the preferential treatment. I think Ben just lost faith in me and didn't believe it was a bike problem. That's why it was so gratifying when I finished second and third just two rounds later at Mallory Park on a Kawasaki.

Incidentally, Ian Simpson was riding a Ducati 748 production bike for the Red Bull Ducati team that year and when I got sacked he was promoted onto my bike. Ian found the same problems I had and was almost in tears of frustration when I spoke to him about it because he couldn't do a thing with the bike the way it was. When John Reynolds crashed and dislocated his shoulder at Mallory Park, the team put pressure on Ian to get results. He said he couldn't do anything unless they made the changes that I had recommended and this time Ben Atkins listened. Surprise, surprise, when the modifications were made Ian started getting some good results including a win at Cadwell Park.

It wasn't the first time I'd been vindicated when it came to my set-up skills. From the first time I rode the Honda RC45 in 1994 I said there was something fundamentally wrong with it because it just wouldn't steer. Of course, no one believed Honda could make a bike that didn't steer so everyone thought it was just me being fussy again. But over the years, Carl Fogarty, Aaron Slight, Niall Mackenzie (who tested one for *Motor Cycle News*), Jim Moodie, Phil Borley and many others came to agree with me – the bike just didn't steer. Jim Moodie rode an RC45 quite a while after I had and I remember him saying, 'Steve Hislop was right about this bike, it doesn't go where you want it to.'

It always feels good to be proved right but it would be even better if people would listen to me at the time. Even way back in 1988 I told Honda my RC30 was selecting false neutrals but they didn't believe me until the bike was stripped and the problem found. It's me that's out on the track with whichever bike I'm riding so no one knows better than I do if it's got a problem. I just wish teams would listen.

It makes me look bad with racing fans too because they probably think I'm just moaning unnecessarily and not trying hard enough and the press don't help when they sensationalize stories of me slating bikes. Hell, it's part of my *job* to diagnose problems with bikes and get them ironed out so why should I be slated for it?

Anyway, when news got out that I had picked up my P45 from the Red Bull team I started getting phone calls from other teams offering me rides. Kawasaki offered me a test on Terry Rymer's bike at Mallory Park, which I accepted and I was on the pace straight away. Terry's team boss, Colin Wright, was impressed enough to offer me a ride at Mallory when Terry was away riding at Suzuka in Japan. He actually wanted me to have some more rides on Terry's spare bike for the rest of the season but Terry refused as he felt he needed both bikes and that was fair enough. Ultimately, it's up to the rider to decide if anyone else can ride their spare bike because it's written into their contract that they will have two bikes at their disposal.

However I still got to race his bike at Mallory and, like I said, I finished on the podium both times which felt great after all the problems I'd had on the Ducati. After that, it was time to join yet another team, this time for the remainder of the season.

My old Devimead Ducati team-mate, Ray Stringer, was running a private Kawasaki team with sponsorship from Sabre Airways and asked if I'd like to join him. He said he couldn't pay me but I was desperate to race and had no other options so I agreed to ride for him.

Our first outing was at Knockhill and I finished second, which was a brilliant result for a private team considering there were so many factory bikes on the grid. I finished fourth in the second leg to prove it wasn't a fluke and the prize money definitely came in handy since I wasn't getting any wages.

I didn't manage to repeat those kind of results

in the last three rounds for various reasons but I still finished in fairly respectable positions for a privateer, ending the season in ninth place overall. That was obviously disappointing considering I'd been the champion just two years before, but I did change teams three times during the season so I couldn't really have expected much more.

I had a good third place in a one-off ride in the Bol d'Or 24 Hour endurance race with Christian Sarron's Yamaha France team and we had a great laugh just hanging out in the South of France. Christian was supposed to be the figurehead of the team but to me he was more like the entertainments manager as he didn't seem to do anything else except keep us all amused. He hired a speedboat one day and we all went cruising on the Med. At one point Christian and I jumped into the sea and swam to a rocky coastline. When I asked him why the others wouldn't come in the water he said, 'Probably because zer are quite a lot of ze sharks round eer.' Shit, I swam back to that boat quicker than Duncan Goodhew and never set foot in the water again.

I rounded off the season at Bishopscourt in Northern Ireland with a win on the Sabre Kawasaki then after that all I could think about was the up-coming birth of my first son. Kelly had been acting weirdly one night back in March and she went out for a while leaving me wondering what the hell was going on. I didn't realize it at the time but apparently Kelly was too scared to tell me she was pregnant because she was so young and didn't know how I'd react to the news. I had never been a big fan of kids but when she came back late that night and plucked up the courage to tell me I was delighted. Me, a daddy? Fantastic! It's funny how you can go through life not being all that bothered about children but when you're told you're going to have one it's such a thrill; I just suppose I'd reached the right time in my life. So from that point on I spent most of my time getting ready to be a dad. I bought a bigger car so I could throw a pram in the boot, I started decorating a nursery in the house and I even went to antenatal classes with Kelly.

We spent a long time thinking about a name but eventually decided on calling our first child Aaron. Everyone thinks I named my son after the World Superbike racer Aaron Slight but that's not the case. I just liked the name and we chose Alexander as his middle name after my dad – who I'm sure would have been very proud to be a grandpa – and my brother Garry whose middle name was Alexander.

Aaron was due on 20 December 1997 but he was five days late and didn't actually arrive until Christmas Day. Kelly was in and out of the hospital for the best part of a week with varying levels of contractions and she ended up being in labour for over 50 hours in total, which must have been a nightmare for the poor girl. I slept on a chair next to her bed in hospital and at 3am on Christmas morning she went into the delivery room and the miracle happened at 8.55am. I was a father.

I was in tears when little Aaron Alexander Hislop

came into this world weighing eight pounds and 10 ounces – I was just completely overwhelmed with emotion. I checked him all over to make sure everything was in working order then I spotted one of his fingers was missing. I told Kelly who had a look, laughed and uncurled the little digit, which had just been folded up out of sight!

That was the best Christmas present I ever had; a healthy baby boy. It's a feeling you can't describe to anyone who hasn't experienced it but having a child is just the greatest thing on earth. When you've got a kid it doesn't matter what other problems you have in your life because they give you so much joy that everything else becomes irrelevant.

Not long before Aaron was born I'd had another surprise when Cadbury's Boost Yamaha team boss, Rob McElnea, called me up out of the blue. He said, 'I know we've had our differences in the past (Rob had refused to give me parts for my short-lived Yamaha team back in 1992) but I hope that's all behind us and I'd like you to ride for the Boost team alongside Niall Mackenzie.'

I thought, 'Fuckin' hell! Me, getting the same bikes as Mackenzie? Wow!' I couldn't believe that I was finally going to get the most competitive bike in the British championship and I'd be riding for the best team too. Mackenzie had already won the title for two years running so I knew the bikes were up to it and I couldn't have been more delighted. Well, actually I could have – if the team had paid me a wage. The catch in the otherwise perfect set-up was that I wouldn't get paid anything because the team couldn't afford it. Chris Walker had ridden for nothing in 1997 so it's not like it was just me being victimized but even so it was a bit of a bummer. Still, as Rob Mac said, he was offering me a shop window in which to get noticed again after two dodgy years of poor results and team fall-outs.

I accepted because I was desperate to get a good bike but it was annoying that my team-mate, Niall Mackenzie, was the best paid guy in the British Superbike paddock and I was getting nothing. I just think I'm not cut out to make any money. I survived that year on prize money and personal sponsorship deals but it should have been a much bigger earner than it was.

Anyway, I agreed terms in December and the next few months were pure bliss with the knowledge that I had the best bike in the country for the following season and a beautiful little baby boy to dote on. Life was good.

The Final Lap

'I can't walk away with a sad exit from Rockingham. I'd like to have a good result somewhere else then call it a day.'

Steve Hislop wasn't unduly worried about being dropped from his MonsterMob Ducati team at the end of the 2002 season. In fact, as a man who quickly became bored with circumstances and routine, he was quite excited about facing a new challenge again once the initial shock had subsided.

While Steve hated the insecurity of not having a job lined up to pay the bills, no one was in any doubt that the reigning British Superbike champion would find a new team before long. Few people, however, thought a man on the wrong side of 40 would attract the interest of a MotoGP world championship team but Hizzy's racing career never did follow the obvious path.

Having secured a highly-prized franchise to run a team in the series again in 2003, the WCM (World Championship Motorsport) squad found themselves without riders as Gary McCoy had signed for Kawasaki while John Hopkins departed to join Suzuki. Unable to secure major sponsorship and factory machinery, the team had decided to build their own four-stroke Grand Prix machine for the coming season and the man that team boss Peter Clifford wanted to ride it was Steve Hislop.

There were many who queried whether 40-year-old Hislop was up for the challenge of a full world championship campaign but his Valentino Rossi-beating lap of Donington Park in the final round of the 2002 British championship proved beyond doubt that he at least still had the talent to challenge the best racers in the world; if he could only find the motivation required to sustain him over a long, arduous season.

Clifford asked his former GP rider Niall Mackenzie what he thought about signing Steve for the season and Mackenzie was quick to support the idea. 'Hizzy's lap of Donington rightfully gained him loads of publicity and convinced Peter that he was still a world class rider on a four-stroke machine. I'm sure he would have done a good job for Peter but I don't think the timing was right. You really need a three year plan in GPs and Steve would have been 41 when the season started so it was perhaps a bit too late for him.'

In the end, despite the sensation the story caused in the biking press, Steve was realistic enough not to be carried away by the flattery of the offer. 'The team didn't have a bike at that point and I didn't think they'd be able to build something competitive in such a short time frame so I wasn't very convinced from a machinery point of view.'

But for Steve there was another, and more important, reason for turning down the offer – his kids. 'It wouldn't have been easy travelling round the world and trying to look after my boys at the same time so that was a big factor for me and, to be honest, I like being at home between races so I don't think MotoGP would have been right for me at that stage in my career.'

While experienced GP campaigner Mackenzie may have expressed some concern over Hislop's age, he had no doubts that Hizzy was world championship material as far as riding skills were concerned but, as he explains, that was only part of the overall package required at world level and he believes Hizzy's attitude may have prevented him securing a Grand Prix ride years before. 'Steve said what he liked when he liked and while that made him such a character, teams and sponsors know what they want to hear from their riders and to get a Grand Prix ride you've got to play the game. Steve's record of inconsistency also worked against him. He was either setting the pace or was miles off it – there was no in between. But when he was on the pace he was awesome; completely flowing, smooth, accurate and right on the edge but able to control everything. He never looked like he was going to fall off.'

With the benefit of hindsight, turning down the WCM team proved to be a wise decision on Steve's behalf as their MotoGP bike was banned from the series for a number of races and suffered numerous technical difficulties.

His professional career may still have been up in the air in October of 2002 but Steve's private life was transformed around the same time when he met a 36-year-old private banker called Ally Greenwood. Having spent the last five months being single following his final estrangement from Kelly Bailey, Steve had almost convinced himself that he wasn't cut out for relationships. They had all failed in the past and, by his own admission, his defence barriers had gone up again.

After talking to all of the major British Superbike teams, Steve finally opted to return to the Virgin Yamaha squad he'd last raced for in 2000. He'd worked well with the team in the past and knew he could fit straight back in again but the big difference for 2003 was that he'd be riding a modified version of Yamaha's R1 road bike rather than the bona fide R7 racer he rode in 2000. Still, Hizzy felt the 1000cc four-cylinder machine would easily be a match for the dominant V-twin Ducatis since new rules for the coming season allowed them to produce more horsepower than before and, besides, Steve Plater had already shown the R1s were capable of winning races having taken two wins towards the end of the 2002 season.

After being dropped from the MonsterMob team so soon after taking the title, Steve was more motivated than ever for 2003 and he was never faster than when he had a point to prove. With a new girlfriend and a new deal signed for the 2003 season, Hizzy could not have been happier and he spent the remainder of the off-season enjoying the company of Ally, her daughter Shannon and his own two boys, Aaron and Connor.

After a winter of romance, Hislop felt refreshed, happy and ready to attack the new season on his Yamaha R1 but right from the word go he was plagued with problems. The Yamaha team had been due to test at Donington Park in the first week of February but when Steve flew in he found the circuit under two inches of snow, cancelling all hopes he had of trying out his new bike. But at that point he was still full of confidence, telling *Motor Cycle News* 'We've got another test booked at Snetterton on 19 March and then we're off to Spain. All I need is half a day to get used to the bike then I'll test some different parts and I'll be ready to race.'

But it wasn't to be so simple. Steve crashed during his first outing on the bike at Snetterton in Norfolk and suffered concussion. More importantly, he lost even more time from the team's already scant pre-season testing programme. 'It was a bit embarrassing really – I just ran into a corner too fast and had to take to the grass. But otherwise the bike felt good and I think I can be competitive on it and maybe even win the title on it.'

Hizzy crashed again in the team's final big test at Valencia in March. Having only crashed twice throughout the entire 2002 season, his record of two accidents before the new season even started did not bode well. This time, however, it wasn't Steve's fault;

he simply ran out of ground clearance when cornering which caused the bike's crank cases to touch down on the track and throw him off. Still, the team had enjoyed three full days of testing before the incident and Steve claimed he was finally comfortable with the bike and happy with the level of front end feel which was so crucial to his high corner-speed riding style.

There was to be just one more outing on the Yamaha before the season started and that was at an official BSB test day at Donington Park in March. For the first time Ally Greenwood got to see what Steve did for a living – and it wasn't altogether a pleasant experience. 'I have never felt so sick in all my life. I was standing alongside the pit wall and my whole body was shaking – and that was just practice. I couldn't walk away though and every time he came round the corner Id think 'Okay, he's made it safely round, that's one less lap to go.'

As the first race of the 2003 season finally got underway at Silverstone, Hizzy's initial pre-season confidence quickly waned. After scoring a win and a second place at the opening Silverstone round in 2002 on his Ducati, Steve could only manage disappointing eighth and fifth positions on the Yamaha this time around. He blamed brake problems for both results: 'I just couldn't stop the thing for the slower corners – it was skipping and juddering all over the place. I was lucky I didn't crash.'

But worse was to come at the Snetterton round in April where Hislop retired from both races saying the bike simply wouldn't handle. Although he had seemed happy with the chassis set-up during the Valencia test, now he couldn't get the Yamaha tuned in to run his trademark high corner-speeds. That Steve was no big fan of the Snetterton circuit didn't help matters but he certainly didn't do himself any favours within his team by abandoning both races. But that was true to form for Hizzy; if the bike wasn't performing as he felt it should be he simply wasn't prepared to risk his neck for anyone or anything, especially for a lacklustre midfield result.

Virgin Yamaha team boss, Rob McElnea, has his own take on why Steve failed to gel with the R1. 'Whenever you sign Hizzy you know there's going to be good times and bad times. I thought the good times would outweigh the bad in 2003 but I realized almost straight away that Steve wasn't clicking with the R1; he crashed twice in practice and that just wasn't like him so it was obvious he was struggling.'

'The Ducati is much more of a corner speed bike – like an overgrown 250cc bike – which suited Steve's style. The four-cylinder machines need to be stopped, turned, and sat up again onto the fat part of the tyre so the rider can get the power down early and that simply wasn't Steve's way of riding and I think he was just too old to adjust to it.

'We did some testing once the season had started and Hizzy was breaking lap records but on a race weekend his riding would deteriorate leading up to race day. I think in a race on the Yamaha he had to take more chances than he was comfortable with and more than he would have had to take on the Ducati.'

However justified Steve's reasons for abandoning those races were to him, they weren't good enough for McElnea who issued Hizzy with a written warning threatening to sack him if he didn't try harder. For some riders this would have been a major cause for concern but Steve was fairly nonchalant about the threat. 'I wasn't too worried because I've been sacked so many times anyway. One more wouldn't have made much difference. But I didn't just give up in those races like some people think. I was trying like hell but the bike was all over the place under braking and it was just really dangerous. It's not like I spat the dummy and ran off in a huff – I went straight back into the garage to debrief the mechanics to try and get the problem sorted for the next round.'

It appeared that McElnea's written warning did, however, have some effect because Hizzy was back on the podium at the following round at Thruxton with a second place in leg one which he followed up with fifth in race two and he was obviously a much happier man for it. 'I knew the Yamaha would be better suited to Thruxton because it's a fast circuit and I'd watched a video of Sean Emmett riding well on the same bike there the year before so I felt I could get a result.'

After struggling again with bike set up at Oulton Park, Hizzy still managed to bag another podium position in the first leg of the two-race meeting but only after Dean Ellison crashed out of third on the last lap, effectively gifting him the position. It wasn't

Steve's best result by any means but it was of great significance nonetheless as it turned out to be the last time he ever stood on a race podium.

Despite the fact that it was his home track, Hislop was never very fond of Knockhill in Scotland – at least on a Superbike. 'It's a nice track for a little 250' he admitted 'but it's just too tight and twisty for the big bikes.' Add to that sentiment the foulest weather conditions encountered in the season so far and it's easy to understand how Steve only managed a dire 13th place in the first leg (and was the last rider not to be lapped) before salvaging at least some pride with fifth in the second. Even so, he was lying in a lowly eighth place overall in the championship standings and realized the chances of retaining his title had all but disappeared.

A fifth and seventh at Brands Hatch were in keeping with Hizzy's poor form on the Yamaha and those who didn't know him wondered why he couldn't get closer to the front of the pack, even if his bike wasn't quite to his liking. After all, his younger and much more inexperienced team-mate Gary Mason was finding some form and proved the point by beating Hislop in both Brands races.

But those who really knew Steve were aware that he was mentally defeated and wasn't prepared to take chances on a bike which wouldn't do what he wanted it to do. Had he been 10 years younger, Steve might just have pushed that bit harder and taken more risks but having become totally disillusioned with the Yamaha he longed for his old thoroughbred racing Ducati which he could tailor so specifically to his needs.

Still, Steve was in good spirits – at least away from the racetrack – going into what would be his last ever meeting at Rockingham, the circuit which had so cruelly robbed him of the BSB title in 2001 when he crashed into a retaining wall and suffered injuries serious enough to put an end to his championship season.

No fan of the track itself and completely hacked off with the Yamaha R1, Hizzy turned in two of the worst performances of his career at Rockingham finishing in 10th and 11th places. It was no surprise to anyone when he parted company with the Yamaha team after the event following a sit-down with Rob McElnea who, analytical as ever, quickly measured up the reasons for Hizzy's dismal performances. 'I think Steve particularly struggled at Rockingham because he'd had a bad crash there before and because all the delays in practice (due to an organizational blunder over white lines being painted on the track) had unsettled him. It's also not the kind of fast, flowing circuit which he liked. After his results there I had to let him go; I've got to answer to Yamaha and my sponsors and the results just weren't good enough so we settled things as amicably as we could and went our separate ways.'

Hizzy himself was more relieved than anything else to be quit of the burden of riding the R1. 'I was glad to be out of the team because I just never felt comfortable with the bike so there was no point in going on. It was best for everyone if we just called it a day.'

One person who was sad to see Steve go was his Virgin Yamaha team-mate Gary Mason. The 24-year-old rider had said at the start of the season that he felt like Luke Skywalker being taught by Yoda in *Star Wars*, such was the difference in experience between the two riders. And even though their working relationship was brief, he felt he had learned at least a few tricks from the old master. 'I really, really liked Steve and even though he wasn't having a great season, he still pulled me aside and taught me so much about racing. He really brought me on in 2003 and said I could go all the way to the top and I desperately want to prove him right to show to everyone that he wasn't wasting his time on me.'

Unsure about whether he would race again in 2004, Hizzy was at least determined that he would not finish his career with such poor results. 'I can't walk away with a sad exit from Rockingham. I'd like to have a good result somewhere else then call it a day. At the end of the day I've had a great career but I wouldn't like to leave it the way it's finished.'

Privately, Steve wished he'd been sacked from Yamaha after the Snetterton round because ETI Ducati team boss, Alastair Flanagan, was keen to get Hizzy back on his title-winning Ducati which he himself was running in 2003 with John Crawford, albeit without much success. Had Hizzy been sacked instead of just receiving a written warning earlier in the year, he may have joined the ETI team in time to successfully defend his title but ultimately it was not to be. Steve did, however, call Flanagan soon after his sacking and was immediately offered a place in the team – on the condition that Sean Emmett approved. Emmett had been sacked from his Renegade Ducati team and was quickly signed up by Flanagan at the expense of Crawford who suddenly found himself without a ride. Due to contractual obligations which state that a rider must have access to two machines, it was Emmett's decision alone whether or not he would be prepared to sacrifice his spare bike by giving it to Hislop and, to his eternal credit, he called Steve personally and told him he could have the bike. Emmett may have fought tooth and nail with Hizzy for the 2002 title but the two remained good friends and his selfless gesture proved him to be a worthy sportsman.

Ally Greenwood knows better than anyone how important Steve's rides on the Ducati were going to be in influencing his career – or retirement. 'Steve was talking about retirement a lot but it all depended on how things went on the ETI Ducati. If he'd had great results on that in the last four races of the season he would probably have done another year; but only if he'd scored three or four wins. If he'd just managed a couple of podiums I think he would have retired. Steve was just trying to prove a point after his disappointing results on the Yamaha.'

Hislop sat out the Mondello Park round of the series because he didn't like the track and wouldn't have had time to test the ETI Ducati but he was amused at the comments made by his former team boss McElnea in *Motor Cycle News*. McElnea had referred to Hislop as an 'enthusiasm hoover' and pointed to Gary Mason's

race-leading performance at Mondello as evidence
that the team were functioning better without Steve's
negative approach. Hizzy quietly made plans to get
his own back at Oulton Park; plans that involved two
grid girls pushing Dyson vacuum cleaners onto the
grid in deference to McElnea's remarks!

Joking aside, the scene was well and truly set for
Oulton Park: Hizzy was to be reunited with his beloved Ducati and would be making his comeback
at his favourite UK track on 10 August. ETI team
manager, Ian Simpson, knew Steve could deliver the
goods – and would fit in perfectly with the squad's no-
nonsense philosophy. 'It was going to be an absolute
honour for the ETI team to have Hizzy riding for us.
Steve was never one for all the corporate bullshit
and after dinner speeches; he just wanted to race and
that's what our team is all about. We're just a little
tight-knit team nowhere near as big as Virgin Yamaha
or Rizla Suzuki but that's the sort of set up Steve liked.
I've no doubt that he'd have been flying at Oulton
Park.'

Fast, open and undulating, Oulton was the closest
thing to a pure road circuit that the BSB series had
to offer and Hizzy loved it. Added to that was the
accepted wisdom that a sacked Hizzy was a frighten-
ingly fast Hizzy and few doubted that he would be
out to prove to his former employers and any other
detractors that he wasn't a spent force; that talent like
his does not disappear overnight. It may have been
too late in the season to have any hopes of retaining
his number one plate but only a fool would have bet

against Hizzy winning a race at Oulton Park. Then it happened.

Shortly after 11am on the morning of 30 July, 2003, the helicopter Steve Hislop was piloting crashed into remote moorland near Teviot Head in Scotland just six miles south west of his old stomping ground of Hawick. It exploded into a massive fireball killing Steve instantly. The world had lost a legend.

To anyone who had ever known Hizzy or watched him race it was, quite simply, incomprehensible. Fatalities amongst motorcycle racers are, unfortunately, all too common and 2003 had been as bleak a year as anyone in the sport could remember. First, popular racer and bike journalist Simon 'Ronnie' Smith had been killed in a road accident in January, and then the legendary Barry Sheene was taken from us by cancer in March. The following month, promising young racer Guy Farbrother was killed in a road accident at just 18 years of age and soon afterwards MotoGP superstar Daijiro Katoh lost his life in the opening round of the season at Suzuka. In June, the fastest ever man around the TT course, David Jefferies, was killed in practice for the 2003 event.

The bike racing world was numbed by the terrible losses it had already suffered but life had to go on. Racers kept racing, teams found other riders to replace those no longer around and the fans continued to turn up at circuits around the world because they all love the sport and they all know the risks.

Whichever way you choose to view it there is no escaping the fact that motorcycle racing is a very dangerous sport and, although safety standards have improved dramatically over the last 20 years, tragedies still do, and will continue to, happen on occasion. It is, quite simply, the nature of the beast. Riders sometimes pay the ultimate price to participate in their sport of choice and all of them are acutely aware that while motorcycle racing offers highs that few other sports can match, it can also provide lows that few other sports can equal.

But the terrible irony in Steve's case was that he was ready to retire from racing after more than 20 years of risking his life in one of the most dangerous sports on earth. He had scored an incredible 11 victories round the TT course, the most unforgiving racetrack in the world, at record speeds, and came away unscathed. He was ready to pack it all in after the 2003 season and dedicate his retirement to bringing up his beloved boys Aaron and Connor.

Sadly, it was never to be but it is of at least some comfort to those closest to Steve that he had come as close to finding true happiness in the last few months of his life as he had ever done, both in his personal life and in his relatively new-found passion for flying helicopters.

After so long racing bikes, no one was unduly worried about Steve's new hobby. He was, by all accounts, a very good pilot and it seemed a harmless way for him to get a buzz after he'd retired from racing. And who could deny him the pleasure when he had repeatedly stated that flying helicopters made him happier than anything else in the world with the exception of his family.

Yet the strangeness and cruelness of this world cannot be measured and on 30 July during what should have been a leisurely pleasure flight from his home town of Hawick down to High Wycombe in Buckinghamshire, the Robinson helicopter he was piloting fell from the sky and claimed the life of a man who had been a hero to thousands, a friend to hundreds, a father to two and a son to one incredibly brave woman who had already endured more suffering than any person should in a lifetime. Whatever way you looked at it, it was a tragedy.

Steve often visited Wycombe Air Park in Buckinghamshire where he was permitted to fly various helicopters belonging to friends. He would have dearly loved to have his own but couldn't justify spending upwards of £100,000 on a toy when he had two young boys to bring up. They always came first.

On Monday 28 July Hizzy borrowed the Robinson four-seater helicopter from a friend at Wycombe and flew around 300 miles north to Hawick in Scotland to visit Andrew Brodie. Brodie had been great friends with Steve ever since they were youngsters and the pair never lost touch even though Steve's commitment to his glittering career meant he couldn't spend much time back in his old neighbourhood. Andrew had been there for Steve from a very early age and he was there as a friend right to the end. He was the last person to see Steve Hislop alive.

'Steve had been talking about flying up to my place ever since he had started flying and when he came up for his grandmother's funeral in June he was standing in my garden looking at the lawn between my conservatory and hedge. He said 'I reckon I could land my helicopter in there you know' and I said 'Piss off, you're not landing a bloody helicopter in my garden.' So I ended up mowing a circle in the field behind the house and I mowed a little path to my garden wall and built a stile over it – it was mock red carpet treatment.'

'Anyway, on the Tuesday night (29 July) Steve took me, his ex-girlfriend Wendy Oliver and a good friend called Jock Hamilton up for a pleasure flight then Steve and I had a great night in my house doing what we did when we were boys – playing folk songs on my guitar and accordion. Steve loved his folk music and we churned out old favourites like *The Fields of France* and *The Fields of Athen Rye*. It was a great night, just like the old days and we sipped a couple of beers in the conservatory as the sun went down. I remember it being a beautiful summer's evening. At one point Steve spread out lots of maps on the floor to plan his route back to High Wycombe the next day and he pointed out all the places he would be flying over.

'On the morning of 30 July Steve came through from the spare room in his pants and T-shirt and went straight to the kitchen window to check out the weather. I distinctly remember him saying 'Look at that fucking weather – it's fucking shite.' Those were his exact words. It was a bit wet and misty but the forecast said the rain would clear from the west so I thought he'd be on his way by lunchtime.

'As I left to go to work at about nine in the morning he said 'I could still be here at dinner time with this weather. In fact I could still be here at fucking tea time.' So I said 'Well, what are we having for our tea then?' and he muttered something about fish and chips. We both walked through my utility room to my garage and I showed him how to shut the electric door from the inside after I'd left. I said 'I'll see you when I see you then' and he replied 'Aye, okay then.'

'My last image of Steve will never leave my mind. As I reversed out of my driveway he was silhouetted against the light from the garage window behind him, grinning and giving me the thumbs up. As he stood like that, the garage door came slowly down like a curtain falling and that was it: that was the last I ever saw of him.'

At approximately 11am, Steve finally left Brodie's house, apparently satisfied that the weather had cleared sufficiently to allow for a safe flight home. Despite his chosen profession, Steve Hislop was not a risk-taker; time and again he had shown he was a perfectionist and anyone who knew him would know that he would not have flown if the conditions were not right.

Shortly after 11am a local farmer, Walter Douglas, noticed a low-flying helicopter passing his farm at Carlenrig just off the A7 between Hawick and Langholm. Like anyone else casually observing a passing helicopter he thought nothing more of it and could never have imagined that the same aircraft would soon be lying in one of his own fields, a smouldering, burned-out shell.

The gentle valley in which the helicopter crashed was so remote and hidden from nearby roads that no one saw or heard anything of the massive fireball which occurred as the machine came down – the fireball which killed one of the most famous motorcycle racers of all time.

It wasn't until several hours later at about 4.30pm that Douglas himself discovered the wreckage while checking his livestock. The first thing he saw were the rotor blades lying on their own in the field but almost immediately afterwards he spotted the smoking wreckage of the Robinson R44 about 100 metres away – a sight which was so incongruous with his peaceful daily routine as to appear surreal. 'I was out on the hills checking my livestock and I spotted some wreckage by the river. I went to investigate and found a small helicopter. It was obvious the accident had happened quite a while beforehand and there was nothing much I could do to help anybody so I went straight back and reported it to the emergency services.'

Police logged Douglas's call at 4.50pm and 10 minutes later two officers from Lothian and Borders divisional headquarters in Hawick arrived at the scene. Upon surveying the scene, the officers immediately called for further assistance and were soon joined by fire engines and ambulances as the crash site was cordoned off and placed under 24 hour guard.

An ambulance later took Hislop's body to a mortuary in Edinburgh for a post-mortem while mountain rescue workers searched the remote area surrounding the crash site for further wreckage.

The Air Accidents Investigation Bureau (AAIB) was informed of the crash as a matter of routine and a three-man team left their base in Farnborough to drive overnight to the crash site, arriving in the early hours of Thursday morning. They were later joined by the Helicopter Manufacturers' European safety and technical investigator, Richard Sanford, who advised on the specifics of the Robinson R44 that Steve had been flying.

On Friday afternoon, two days after the crash, the helicopter wreckage was taken to Farnborough for forensic investigation and the AAIB announced that it could take four to six months before the exact cause of the accident was known. Without any eye witnesses to the accident and with very little left of the burned-out helicopter to analyse, it was immediately clear that this was going to be a difficult and prolonged case.

Predictably, rumours concerning the cause of the crash spread like wildfire as people scrambled to make at least some sense of what was a senseless tragedy. One of the most widely discussed theories was that military jets and a military Chinook helicopter were operating in the area and could have been involved in some manner. The downwash from a jet engine could easily be enough to destabilise a small helicopter but initial reports suggested that there were no jets in the area at the time of Hislop's accident. Others claimed the weather was poor and suggested that Steve should perhaps not have flown at all but Andrew Brodie insists conditions were dry with high cloud cover by mid-morning, around the time when Steve would have taken off. The only real fact known is that nothing will be certain until the AAIB publish their final report, whenever that may be.

One theory which angered those who knew Steve was the doubt expressed by some over his ability to fly the type of helicopter he was flying. Steve's close friend, fellow racer and fellow helicopter pilot Jim Moodie is just one well-qualified commentator who pours scorn on any such notion. Hislop had intended to fly up to Glasgow to visit Moodie on 29 July but when he called, Moodie told him he would be testing with his Valmoto Triumph team at Cadwell Park and would not be at home so the visit was cancelled. Moodie owns his own Robinson R44 – the same model of helicopter which Steve was flying at the time of his accident – and Hizzy had flown that too, very competently according to Moodie. 'What they said in the press about him not being experienced enough to fly that model was rubbish. I've been up with Steve and he was a very good pilot and had flown plenty of hours in the R44 – he had lots more hours in it in than the law required (the law required a minimum of five hours while Steve had racked up 22 hours in that specific model). Some people claimed the Robinson was too nervous and responsive for a pilot of Steve's experience but it's not at all. Steve was perfectly well qualified to fly that helicopter.'

Only time and extensive forensic analysis will reveal exactly what caused the crash and until that information has been published, further speculation is futile. But while it is important to know exactly what happened on Steve's last flight, it is of largely academic importance to those closest to him since the end result is the same: they have lost the man they loved and admired.

Mercifully, Aaron and Connor may comprehend little and remember little of the loss of their father; such is the resilience of young children. Ally was staying with a friend in Northern Ireland and hadn't heard from Steve all morning.

'That was unusual for us because we used to call and text all the time. I obviously couldn't call him because he was flying but when I got a text from Wendy Oliver asking if I'd heard from Steve I started to panic. I rang Mike Wilds, a helicopter instructor at Wycombe and a good friend of Steve's, to ask if he'd heard anything. He said he hadn't but told me not to worry.'

'My friend Maureen called the Scottish and Irish police but they didn't know anything. Then Mike called again and he spoke really quietly. He told me again there had been an incident but didn't come straight out with any details. It was only when I pushed him that he said 'The boy's no longer with us.'

Despite her own deep grief, Ally was a tower of strength for the one woman who had lost everything: Margaret Hislop, Steve's beloved mum. It is difficult to imagine one person having endured more grief than Margaret Hislop has with such dignity over the years. To lose her husband at such a young age (he was only 43 at the time of his death) was bad enough; to lose her 19-year-old son Garry just three years later was almost unthinkable and now, to lose her last remaining son just when he seemed at his happiest, would have been beyond the endurance of many a lesser woman.

Margaret had been holidaying in Ladron Bay in Devon with Steve's sons when the tragedy occurred. She could not be traced by police until the early hours of the morning since she was booked into a holiday camp under her partner's name of Hardy rather than her own name of Hislop.

It wasn't until the early hours of Thursday, 31 July, that police finally traced Margaret and George to deliver the news that every parent dreads and by that point the news had been leaked and broadcast with a shameful lack of respect for Steve's family. Steve had always considered his mother to be the strongest woman he had ever known because of the way she coped with the loss of Sandy and Garry. Margaret had shown a strength and dignity beyond belief during – and long after – those terrible times and had always been very close to Steve because of their shared loss. Now, unbelievably, Margaret Hislop was to be tested again in a way that no mother should ever have to be tested. Her only surviving son had been killed leaving her alone out of a once happy family of four.

Her grief at hearing the news of Steve's death can only be imagined but the only thing which kept

Margaret going was the false hope that the police had made a mistake. 'I remember I kept asking them if they were sure it was my Steven and they kept saying 'yes.' I simply couldn't believe that it had happened again.'

Knowing they would never sleep that night, Margaret and George left Devon around 2am and drove through the night back to their home in Denholm near Hawick with Steve's two boys sound asleep in the back of the car, still blissfully unaware of the tragedy which had struck.

Margaret Hislop is a resilient woman and, with the strong support of her tight-knit rural Scottish community and her partner George, she will surely pull through once again as she has done twice before in the face of huge adversity. Her memories of her most famous son, right to the end, are fond ones, made fonder still by the new-found contentment she noticed in Steve during the last months of his life.

'Steven came back to Hawick for his grandmother's funeral on 13 June and for some reason after the burial he wanted to go back up to look at the flowers. That wasn't like Steven so I was quite surprised but I went back up there with him. As he was standing at the graveside, I noticed for the first time that he looked really, really like his father Sandy. I don't know why but there was just something about him that day – he looked different.

'He stood in the cemetery and looked out over the hills and fields and started talking about his childhood. He was telling me that his brother Garry and him used to ride their bikes away over through the trees and that they knew they would be in trouble if their dad had ever found out because it was so far away.'

'Then he started to talk about his dad and he had never really talked about Sandy with me up till then. But that day he talked about them both so much and I'd just never heard him talk like that before. But he seemed so happy with his life and so at peace with himself. It's strange but there was just something different about him that day both in the way he looked and the way he was talking. All that time he was talking to me, Steven was standing on the very spot where he now lies.'

'The last time I ever saw my son was when I was taking his boys for a holiday in Devon. Steven brought Aaron and Connor over from the Isle of Man and George and I met them at a Travel Lodge at Burton-wood near Liverpool. George and I arrived after Steve and the boys and we could hear them all along the corridor playing daft games in their room. I could hear Steven shouting 'You're cheating, you wee monkey' and they sounded like they were having a great time. That night we had a meal and a few drinks and the boys decided to stay in the room with George and I. Steven said to them 'What? Are you leaving me to stay in that room all by myself?'

'After breakfast Steve got into his hire car because he was going down to Wycombe to fly his helicopter and we got in our car to drive to Devon. We followed him for about an hour on the motorway but then we

were due to branch off to go our own way leaving
Steven to go his. Just before we did, he drove right
up alongside our car and smiled and waved at his
boys. They waved back and that was the last we ever
saw of him.'

A Scottish Hero

'If I die young then I've still packed in more than most would do in two lifetimes.'

It is a sad fact of life that we do not always let people know how much they are loved and respected while they are still with us. But if ever a measure was needed to prove the high esteem in which Steve Hislop was held by his colleagues, friends, family, fellow motorcyclists and his local townsfolk, his funeral proved it beyond question.

Thousands of mourners descended on the small town of Hawick in the tranquil Scottish Borders on 7 August, 2003 to pay their final respects to Robert Steven Hislop. They had been gathering from all over the country since 7am to pay their respects in a town many had only heard of because Steve put it on the map.

The service took place at Teviot Parish Church at 12.30pm and every one of the 600 pews were taken up as the congregation listened to hear Hizzy's close friends Jim Davidson and Allan Duffus pay moving tributes to their fallen friend.

'When I think of Steve,' Duffus read, 'I think of a hero. He was a boy who dealt with the sudden loss of Sandy, his father, and he handled it like a hero. He also dealt with the tragic passing of his brother Garry at 19. Again, he handled it like a hero. He was a TT legend but he was more than that. He was a loving father to Aaron and Connor, son to Margaret, friend to most of the people here today and an inspiration to everyone.'

Davidson, a member of the comedy motorcycle stunt group The Purple Helmets which Steve occasionally performed with, provided a welcome relief from the sadness and tension with some heart-lifting tales of Steve's down-to-earth attitude and sense of humour. The following is an extract from the Eulogy penned by Davidson which he read out at the funeral service.

'I remember the time when Steve rang up to go out for a beer and offered to pick me up in his latest set of wheels. I couldn't believe my eyes when this thing appeared outside my house. It was an old Mazda pick-up. It did 20mpg on fuel and 10mpg on engine oil. The newest and most expensive thing on it was his personalised number plate! When I got in, there was cardboard holding the side window in place, and a piece of chewing gum on the dashboard from the previous owner. But at least it had air- conditioning – a huge hole in the floor! But Steve didn't care about material things or what other people thought. It was just a mode of transport to him.'

Davidson also explained his own personal theory

as to why Hizzy stopped racing on the Isle of Man TT circuit and once again, lightened the sombre atmosphere in a manner of which Steve would have fully approved.

'One Saturday afternoon in the depths of winter we'd just finished a mountain bike ride. It was freezing cold, it was dark, and we were soaked to the skin, and as some of you will know, Steve had poor circulation so he was suffering more than most. He was frozen to the bone so he hastily tied his bike onto his car-rack, then stripped all his wet riding clothes off, and drove home naked. His theory was that he would warm up quicker that way. Anyway, everything was going according to plan until he was rounding Windy Corner on the TT course. He casually glanced in his rear view mirror to see his mountain bike bouncing along the road behind him. Quick as a flash he stopped the car, reversed back along the road, and jumped out to retrieve the bike. Just as he was about to tie the bike back onto the car, he was caught in the full glare of an approaching vehicle's headlights. He later said 'I was stranded in the middle of the road like a startled rabbit and I couldn't think what to do so I just smiled and waved at the people in the car'. This must have been one of his scariest moments on the TT course. So the truth is that Steve was probably too embarrassed to ride at the TT ever again'.

As the hundreds who could find no place in the church listened to the service via speakers rigged up outside in the sweltering heat of an August day, the Reverend Neil R Combe aptly summed up Steve's attitude towards life. 'We live in a world where McDonald's is sued because it makes its coffee hot, where a jar of peanut butter has a label on it saying 'Warning – may contain nuts.' Someone like Steve opens our eyes to a bigger world, a world of exciting possibilities for those who are willing to take that calculated risk.'

The church may have been full to bursting but it was only when the hearse moved off towards South-dean cemetery that the sheer scale of the turnout could be witnessed by those who had been inside for the service. It was estimated that up to 1000 bikes followed the hearse through the streets of Hawick on Steve's last journey. The cortege took a full 10 minutes to pass through Hawick's narrow main street on the first leg of the 13 mile route to Hizzy's final resting place.

The only other time the sleepy little town had witnessed anything like it was way back in 1937 when more than 2000 people lined the streets to pay tribute to another motorcycle racing hero, Jimmy Guthrie. The six times TT winner had been an inspiration to the young Steve Hislop and he had always been proud of the fact that he'd met Guthrie's son in 1987.

Steve's mother Margaret was utterly amazed at the scale of the event and was truly humbled at the outpouring of affection and respect for her eldest son. 'I had no idea of the reaction there was going to be to Steven's death. I thought I was just burying my son so I told the undertakers that I wanted the service to be held in the small church in Denholm. He told me that it was never going to be big enough and that was when the wheels started turning in my mind. It was only then that I realized I wasn't just burying my son; that this was going to be something else. When the undertakers suggested having the service in Teviot Church because it was bigger and was next to a big car park where they could place speakers it really started to sink in.'

'The flowers and cards and tributes that started pouring in were just unbelievable. I couldn't believe how many there were; it was staggering and that helped so much in coming to terms with things, just knowing how much Steve was loved. But I could never have got through the whole thing without Steve's girl-friend Ally Greenwood. Ally, Wendy Oliver, Andrew Brodie, Jock Hamilton, Rae Oliver and my partner George. I wouldn't have been anywhere without them. George helped an awful lot as did all the villagers in Denholm and I just can't thank them all enough.'

'After the service I was asked if I minded all the motorcycles following the family cars and I said 'No, of course not' but I was thinking there would maybe be about 20 or 30 bikes. I had no idea what was going on outside the church. When we saw the bikes there were hundreds and hundreds of them. It was just unbelievable. Steven would have been so proud of such a send-off.'

It was a send-off which completely shattered the old stereotyped image of bikers as uncaring, disrespectful hooligans. Grown men in supposedly macho bike leathers wept openly as the hearse passed by the thousands of mourners who lined the streets. The spectacle prompted Chief Superintendent Watson

McAteer of Lothian and Borders Police to tell *Motor Cycle News* 'I've seen nothing like it in 34 years of policing. The dignity and respect shown towards Steve in people's behaviour was amazing. The respect in which he was held was shown in the number and quality of the people who were here today.'

Quality was the right word. Despite the remoteness of the location and the fact that the following day was the first day of practice for the Oulton Park round of the British Superbike championship, everyone connected with the series turned up to pay their last respects. Former rivals including Niall Mackenzie, Shane Byrne, Michael Rutter, Sean Emmett, Jim Moodie and Steve Plater respectfully attended as did Hizzy's former team bosses, Rob McElnea and Paul Bird, alongside many other famous faces from the sport Steve had dedicated his life to.

Ordinary fans, many wearing replicas of Hizzy's distinctive yellow racing helmet, also showed a quiet dignity and respect that was genuinely touching. As the cortege left Hawick for Southdean cemetery, few failed to miss the symbolic significance of the scene: Steve Hislop was leading a pack of pursuing motorcycles for one last time. He was at the front where he was accustomed to being – a winner to the very end. Leader of the pack.

Racing hero he may have been to countless thousands of fans but the floral wreath in the hearse simply reading 'Daddy' was a poignant reminder that Steve was also a loving father to two young boys who had idolized him and who would now have to grow up without a dad, something no young child should have to do.

Robert Steven Hislop was finally laid to rest in Southdean cemetery at 2.50pm alongside his brother Garry and his father Sandy. He was 41 years old. The stillness in the cemetery was overwhelming in the blistering temperatures. The only sounds which could be heard were the twittering of birds and the creaking of leather as hundreds of motorcyclists filed into the cemetery to see off their hero. Family friend Tim Douglas read this self-penned poem at Steve's graveside:

> Today, all the Border so sad is,
> Our summertime shaded with gloom,
> As we mind of two naughty wee laddies,
> As bright as the heather in bloom.
> Brave hearts, strong limbs and young faces,
> In days when the future was bright,
> The thrills and spills of great races,
> As fast as the falcon in flight.
>
> So skilful his hand on the throttle,
> Adrenalin flowing with ease,
> Hard work, dedication and bottle,
> That brought home 11 TTs.
> At home among friends or with strangers,
> For this was one hell of a man,
> Who mastered the worst of its dangers,
> And conquered the Isle of Man.

Our thoughts are with Margaret, his mother,
And two little laddies bereaved,
Who, when they grow up will discover,
The greatness their father achieved.
Fate strikes and its stroke is uneven,
What grief must a heart thole?
First Sandy, then Garry, now Steven,
Dull knives in a fond mother's soul.

On slabs made of marble or granite,
His name will be chiselled with pride,
And when folks in years to come scan it,
They will wonder at why Steven died.
Farewell to a brave Border callant,
In tune with his racing machine,
Who conquered the world with his talent,
And comes home to sleep in Southdean.

The funeral was only the start of the tributes to Steve Hislop. Around the country, and indeed the world, people were paying their respects in a variety of ways, all trying desperately to come to terms with the loss of their hero.

Flags at racetracks across the nation, including Knockhill in Scotland, Oulton Park in England and on the TT course on the Isle of Man, were lowered to half mast. Internet message and chat boards were inundated with moving tributes and messages of condolence, and tributes were paid on various television channels including BBC Grandstand, Men and Motors and Border News – Hizzy's local station both when he lived in the Borders and on the Isle of Man.

But amongst the most moving tributes came at the Oulton Park round of the British Superbike championship immediately after Steve's funeral. Hizzy was, and in a certain sense always will be, the reigning BSB champion. Unable to defend his title, it will be his for eternity and his colleagues and fans did him proud over the Oulton Park weekend just as they had at his funeral.

Every rider taking part in the Superbike class wore a black armband in memory of Steve and also carried 'Hizzy Number 1' stickers on their bikes. The number one pit lane garage was allocated as a shrine to Steve and his 1992 TT-winning Norton was placed on display there with a single red rose resting on the fuel tank. Fans left countless floral tributes in the garage over the weekend and the crowd held aloft hundreds of Scottish Saltire flags simply proclaiming 'Hizzy.'

Before the start of the first Superbike race, Steve's Norton was wheeled out to sit at the front of the grid for a minute's silence in honour of the reigning British champion. Millions of television viewers around the country watched and reflected in silence upon the career of the man they'd become accustomed to seeing riding like the wind, fearless, skilful and courageous to the end. Only the hardest of hearts could have failed to be moved by the occasion.

A new chicane at the track was to be named after Hizzy (the owners of Knockhill have similar plans to name a corner in his memory) and, fittingly, his former team-mate and good friend, Stuart Easton, officially opened it by riding round it on Steve's white Norton.

Easton was nervous about the ceremony but deeply proud to be involved. 'I felt massively honoured when Steve's mum Margaret and his girlfriend Ally asked me if I would ride his TT-winning Norton round Oulton Park to officially open Hizzy's chicane – even though it was a scary experience. I'd never ridden a bike like that and I was really scared of dropping it because it's so special. It didn't help that it was pouring with rain and the bike had ancient cut slicks on it but I was really up for doing it and I managed to keep the bike upright. It really was a great honour.'

For Easton, Hizzy had been more than just a good friend; he had been an inspiration and a true mentor. 'I first met Hizzy at Knockhill in 1995, the year he won the BSB title. I was doing schoolboy motocross at the time but watching him inspired me to take up road racing. Steve helped me straight away with advice on bike set up and riding techniques and he also gave me little bits and bobs like knee sliders and stuff. Even though he was incredibly busy he always took time out to help me and I'll never forget that. Everything I learned from him I still make use of to this day and always will do.'

'Steve really taught me how to be more relaxed about my racing. He said I didn't need to eat lettuce leaves and spend my life down the gym and he taught me to relax before a race, saying that whatever was going to happen was going to happen and that worrying about it wouldn't change things. Now I can sit on the grid and look at other riders shifting from foot to foot and getting all wound up while I'm totally relaxed and that's all Steve's doing.'

'When he split from the MonsterMob team I missed his guidance and would sometimes sneak round to the Yamaha garage to ask him things. For example, I was having problems with my suspension at Thruxton in 2003 and asked my team-mate Shane Byrne for advice. He was having the same problems but couldn't really explain why so I asked Steve and he told me precisely what the bike was doing and how to fix it. I made the changes and they worked perfectly.'

'When Steve used to come past me in testing I would often abort my lap no matter how quickly I was going and just sit up on my bike to watch him for a couple of corners to try and learn something. He was inch-perfect and his lap times showed that; they were so consistent all day long when he was on it. He was incredibly smooth but so fast with it.'

'I'll remember Steve not only as a great racer but also as a great family man. All the advice he gave me will stay with me for the rest of my career. When I have a bad day I just think to myself 'Well, how would Hizzy deal with this?' and I can almost hear him saying 'Get yer bloody finger oot fella and get on with it.'

To ensure he will always be remembered, a Steve Hislop Memorial Fund was initiated soon after his death with the aim of raising the finances to commission two statues of him; one to be erected in Hawick (close to the statue of Hawick's other motorcycling legend Jimmy Guthrie) and the other to be placed at an as-yet undesignated spot on the Isle of Man where Steve not only made his name but lived happily for the last 12 years of his life.

Many events were held to raise the necessary money including a fund-raising night on the Isle of Man, a motorcycle ride-out in the Scottish Borders, a memorial track day at Cadwell Park and an evening auction event in Kelso near Hawick to name but a few. Countless fans who were unable to attend any of these events sent cheques to the fund along with notes of condolence to Steve's family. It is probably fair to say that Steve would have been stunned by the reaction of so many people to his passing for he truly didn't realize just how much he was loved and respected.

Another permanent memorial to Hizzy will be housed in the Duchess room of Drumlanrig Towers in Main Street, Hawick. Steve's trophies, helmets and leathers as well as his first 125cc race bike will be housed there from March 2004 alongside other mementoes from his glittering career. The Summerland leisure complex on the Isle of Man is also hoping to have a Hizzy room displaying memorabilia in the not-too-distant future.

But the best mementoes of Steve Hislop are not trophies, helmets or leathers, they are memories; memories not only of a loving father and devoted son, but of one of the greatest motorcycle racers who ever lived. Results don't always tell the full story of a rider's career and this was never truer than in Steve's case. His career CV lacks only one thing and that is a world championship title, yet few doubt that Steve was easily capable of beating the best in the world on his day as he proved by setting pole position at the Donington Park World Superbike round in 2001 and by lapping the same circuit faster than four-times world champion Valentino Rossi the following year.

So why was he never a world champion? Why did the ultimate accolade escape such a talented rider? It is the last great unanswered question about Steve's life and it seems that everyone has their own opinion on the subject which, when taken together, seem to converge on the same salient points. Hizzy's good friend Jim Moodie offers up his own theory: 'Steve was definitely good enough to have been a world champion. In fact, I'd say that he was the most talented rider never to have been a world champion. There's a lot of people who have been world champions who were never as good as him and there's been a lot of talk about why he never got that break but I don't think it had anything to do with him speaking his mind like most people think – I've always spoken my own mind and it's never done me any harm in getting rides. I think it was more to do with his temperament; he was either in the mood to race or he wasn't and I could tell straight away, either on the phone or in person, if he was in the mood to win. If he was all animated and talking at 100 miles an hour then I knew he was going to win because when he was excited and wound up like that he was practically unbeatable. During qualifying for the 2001 World Superbike round at Donington I told Niall Mackenzie (who was commentating on the event) that Hizzy was going to get pole after talking to him and sure enough he did. But if he was down in the mouth and not saying much I knew he wasn't going to be anywhere.'

As a multiple Isle of Man TT winner himself, Moodie also knows what it takes to win round the most demanding racetrack in the world and he is still in awe as he remembers Hislop's ability round that track. 'Steve was the most awesome racer I ever saw round the TT course – bar none. He just had the complete package of track knowledge, smoothness and speed. It was incredible to watch him round there.'

Hizzy's fierce rival from his British Superbike days, John Reynolds, was equally in awe of Steve's ability at the TT having witnessed it at close quarters. 'I remember racing in my only ever TT in 1989. I entered Barregarrow which is a very fast downhill section where the bike's suspension bottoms out and as far as I was concerned I was going flat out until Stevie came past me like I was standing still. Sparks flew off his bike as the suspension bottomed out and he shot off into the distance towards Kirkmichael with the bike shaking its head all over the place. I thought there and then that if that's what you have to do to win a TT then it's not for me.'

Rob McElnea may have been forced to let Hizzy go from his Virgin Yamaha team in 2003 but few people recognized Steve's talents as acutely as he did. 'I first worked closely with Steve in 1998 when I managed him and Niall Mackenzie in the Cadbury's Boost Yamaha team and it was obvious that his talent then was just so untapped and wasted. He was already 37 years old and pretty much not going to go anywhere else other than the British championship and I could see that was such a great shame. I got lucky enough to race in Grands Prix as did Niall Mackenzie, and Carl Fogarty went World Superbike racing and won four world titles but Hizzy was probably better than all of us; he was definitely better than I was. He was a natural rider and if he'd had the opportunities that Niall, Carl and I had I think it would have been a different case.'

'The guy was totally, 100 per cent committed once he knew where he stood with the bike and the track and the settings. If things were right he rode on pure confidence and could ride perfect laps time after time, way more than the rest of us could ever do. Most riders manage one or two near-perfect laps during a race weekend but Steve could churn them out all day long when he wanted to. He was focused to the point of being mad.'

'There's no question that Steve could have gone a lot further than he did. He certainly had the riding ability but unfortunately it's not just about that. To be a world champion you've got to take the knocks and still be able to perform; you've got to say the right things and do every part of the job that's expected of you. Steve hated all that corporate stuff – he only wanted to ride the bike but you just can't do that any more. Maybe 20 years ago he could have gotten away with it but not now. It's a shame because I really believe he could have been a world champion.'

Michael Rutter, another of Steve's former BSB rivals shares the same sentiment. 'He was the fastest bloke in the world. On his day no one could beat him. Anyone will tell you that; the bloke was so fast, so bang-on line, he just didn't put a foot wrong.'

And Ian Simpson, who would have been Hizzy's team manager had Steve lived long enough to take on the ETI Ducati ride, is yet another believer that Hislop's career potential was never quite fulfilled. As an old friend, he also respected Hizzy's down-to-earth approach to life. 'I knew Steve when he was still working as a mechanic and I was a van driver. He later became a superstar in everyone else's eyes but never in his own. He was one of the best in the world on his day – nobody could touch him. He was absolutely something special. The only reason he never got a chance at world level is that he was just too temperamental. One day he'd be half a lap in front of everybody else and the next weekend he'd be nowhere. I don't know why that was and I don't even think Steve knew why that was. I suppose it's just human nature – nobody's perfect.'

'In my opinion Steve was the best racer ever round the TT without doubt. Nobody could touch him round there and, having thought about it, I think I know why now. Basically, he could go to any short circuit race and within five minutes of the first session he'd be about five seconds quicker than anyone else. Other riders had to work up to speed but Steve's ability to ride a bike fast round those first few corners without any warm-up time was amazing and that worked so well on the pure road circuits like the Isle of Man. At the TT you don't get many practice laps so you're just riding the course as you see it and Steve could do that better than anyone else. He had an uncanny ability to judge racing lines, weather conditions, what the bike was capable of and just to judge how fast he could go under any given circumstances.'

'But that had its downsides too as far as concentration went. Steve would always be fast in Friday practice but by Saturday or Sunday it was almost like he was bored. If you do 150 laps a day of a circuit over two or three days it's easy to see how some people would get bored; again it's just human nature. I think sometimes you can do too much racing and while some riders never seem to suffer from that I think Steve did. It's like any job though; if you do it too much you get sick of it.'

'But that's of no importance now. All that matters is that two young boys have lost their dad and a mother has lost her son. Anyone who knew Steve even a little bit knows what a big softy he was and how much he loved his kids. His death was a real tragedy.'

A corporate hat may never have sat comfortably upon Steve Hislop's head but he would have made a great mentor for younger racers, such was his eagerness to help them avoid the pitfalls that he was all too aware he'd fallen into himself. Almost every rider in the BSB paddock will testify to having been helped by Hizzy at some stage. Shane Byrne, the man who succeeded Steve as BSB champion in 2003 is just one of them. He told TV's *Men & Motors* programme: 'When

I first moved onto a Superbike in 1999 Steve was so helpful to me. He used to make a point of coming over to see how I was getting on because he was on the same bike as me so he'd run through what gearing he was using and suggest different tyres to try. He was just an absolutely spot-on bloke and I always said I'd love to have him as a team-mate and I believe he said the same sort of thing about me.'

Hizzy's titanic battle with his team-mate and fellow Scotsman Niall Mackenzie in 1998 provided one of the most intense and thrilling BSB seasons ever witnessed. The pair fought out a war of words in the press and a war of attrition on the racetrack but all differences were immediately forgotten when Mackenzie heard the dreadful news of Steve's death. 'When Steve died it completely changed the way I thought about him. He irritated me at racetracks but with hindsight I realize it was only because he was pushing me so hard on the track and I didn't like that because I was so used to winning. I just wish he was here to irritate me now. The saddest thing is that Steve never realized how much respect other riders had for him. Everyone looked up to him as a rider but he just wasn't aware of it. He definitely had enough pace and talent to win a world championship but unfortunately that didn't happen.'

There can be no greater accolade than the respect of your peers and it is clear that Hizzy had the full respect and admiration of every last one of his racing colleagues even if, as Mackenzie suggests, Steve himself never quite realized it. But he would have been

even more stunned to hear of the illustrious company
with which he was posthumously compared to.

Whilst celebrating the life and achievements of
Steve Hislop at his funeral, the Reverend Neil R
Combe compared Hizzy with two of Scotland's greatest heroes – Robert the Bruce and William Wallace.
Highbrow historians may have frowned at the com-
parison with a modern motorcycle racer but anyone
who ever had the privilege to know Steve or to watch
him race would not disagree with Combe's sentiment. Motorcycle racing may only be a sport rather
than a matter of national importance but the qualities
needed to compete at Steve's level were the same as
those required by the heroes of antiquity; intelligence,
fearlessness, skill and courage.

Many times Steve came back from horrific injuries
to continue the fight against his rivals; he simply
refused to lie down, roll over or give up. Muscling a
fearsome 190mph motorcycle around the TT course
takes as much courage as facing any enemy in battle
and Steve repeatedly proved that he was better than
any opponent in the world at his chosen, and dangerous, profession. His natural skill on a bike combined
with his lightning fast reactions and keen intelligence
made him a fearsome opponent on any track and on
any machine. He may have been accused of surrender-
ing on occasion but it is only wise men who know
when a battle cannot be won. If there was ever a fighting chance of victory, then Steve fought like a man
possessed, with a passion and determination which
will never be known or experienced by most of us.

In motorcycle racing as in battle, the risks are high and lives are inevitably lost. Steve's skill on a motorcycle ensured he never became another racing casualty. Instead he was taken from us in a tragic accident during a leisurely pleasure trip. After spending years cheating death at frightening speeds on some of the most powerful racing motorcycles in the world, the manner of his death was the greatest of ironies.

But it has been said that as long as a person lives on in the memories of others then he will never truly die. There can be no doubt that countless thousands will pass on tales of Steve Hislop's achievements to new generations ensuring that his life's work and his character will be remembered forever. Whatever the opinion of crusty academics, Hizzy rightfully deserved to be compared to two of Scotland's greatest ever warriors. He was a true Scottish hero.

From his friend and mentor, Wullie Simpson, Steve picked up the phrase 'We're all going to die if we live long enough.' It may sound morbid but it is a stark truth and Steve had a realistic enough grasp on life not only to live by the expression but to read into the humour and irony of it. He fully accepted the risks of his chosen profession and refused to be intimidated by them even when motorcycle racing claimed the life of his younger brother Garry. Likewise, Hizzy accepted the risks involved in flying helicopters and was never happier than when he was at the controls of an aircraft. 'It's like riding a motorcycle in the sky' he once said, beaming at the thought of it even when he was standing on terra firma.

It is true that everybody dies but it is equally true that not everyone really lives. In his own words, Robert Steven Hislop packed more into his 41 years than most people would in two lifetimes so no one should grieve for a life that was wasted. Hizzy lived in the fast lane from a very early age, not just when he was racing a motorcycle at phenomenal speeds but in every aspect of his life. He enjoyed countless triumphs and endured incredible heartache in almost equal measures and always with the greatest dignity – a trait he must have learned from his mother Margaret.

Steve's parting quote for the first edition of this book was 'You ain't seen nothing yet' and it's a quote which has become strangely prophetic. If there is life after death, we can all rest assured that Steve Hislop will be living it to the full – just as he always did.

BARRY SHEENE
1950–2003 The Biography
STUART BARKER

ISBN: 0-00-716181-6

The definitive life story of the seventies world 500cc
motorcycle champion Barry Sheene, the Brit whose
death-defying crashes and playboy lifestyle made him
the most famous bike racer on the planet.

Written by the only journalist to have ridden on the roads
with him, and featuring interviews with closest friends,
team mates and former rivals, this is the complete portrait
of perhaps the greatest circuit racer of them all.

'He's machismo on hot wheels, with irresistible cheek.'
Daily Telegraph

Out now in paperback at all good bookshops

CollinsWillow
An Imprint of HarperCollinsPublishers

www.harpercollins.co.uk

NIALL MACKENZIE
The Autobiography
NIALL MACKENZIE, with STUART BARKER

ISBN: 0-00-714509-8

TWO WHEELS
ONE MAN
NO COMPARISON

Former British Superbike Chmpion and Grand Prix
veteran Niall Mackenzie's entertaining and insightful
autobiography, updated with his latest adventures
both on and off the track.

Out now in paperback at all good bookshops

CollinsWillow
An Imprint of HarperCollinsPublishers

www.harpercollins.co.uk